P9-DFX-822

FOUR PUPPET PLAYS
PLAY WITHOUT A TITLE
THE DIVAN POEMS and OTHER POEMS
PROSE POEMS and DRAMATIC PIECES

by Federico García Lorca

translated by Edwin Honig

The Sheep Meadow Press
Riverdale-on-Hudson, New York

Copyright © 1990 by Edwin Honig and the heirs and beneficiaries of Federico García Lorca

All rights reserved. No part of this publication may be reproduced or transmitted in any form or by any means, electronic or mechanical, including photocopy, recording, or any information storage and retrieval system, without permission in writing from the publisher.

All inquiries and permission requests should be addressed to: The Sheep Meadow Press, P.O. Box 1345, Riverdale-on-Hudson, New York 10471.

Distributed by Consortium Book Sales & Distribution, Inc.
        287 East 6th Street, Suite 365
        St. Paul, MN 55101

Typesetting by Keystrokes, Lenox, Massachusetts
The book was composed in Mergenthaler ITC New Baskerville

Library of Congress Cataloging in Publication Data

García Lorca, Federico, 1898–1936.
  [Poems. English. Selections]
  The divan / Federico García Lorca : new versions by Edwin Honig.
    p. cm.
  ISBN 0-935296-94-8
  I. Honig, Edwin. II. García Lorca, Federico, 1898–1936. Diván del Tamarit.
English. 1990. III. Title.
  [PQ6613.A763A25 1990]
  861'.62—dc20   90-30111
                                                     CIP

Printed in the United States of America

FOUR PUPPET PLAYS
PLAY WITHOUT A TITLE
THE DIVAN POEMS and OTHER POEMS
PROSE POEMS and DRAMATIC PIECES

CONTENTS

OTHER POEMS

INTRODUCTION

It is true that the experimental Lorca of the unfinished last play *The Public* and the earlier *When Five Years Pass* (1931) is quite different from the Lorca of the great tragedies, *Blood Wedding, Yerma,* and *The House of Bernarda Alba,* all written in a few years (1931–1935). But it is also true that the four farces and prose poems *(narraciones),* written variously from 1922 to 1934, contain innovations he was trying out as much as in his more obvious experimental work. Similarly, in the group of twenty-one poems known as the *Divan of the Tamarit,* composed on his return to Andalusia after visiting North and South America in 1929 and 1934, folk spirit and surrealist imagery jostle one another through traditional poetic forms.

As in his *Gypsy Ballads* and *Poem of Deep Song,* Lorca was replenishing a many-layered cultural heritage of Greco-Roman, Byzantine, Arabic, Hebrew, old Iberian, and Visigothic civilizations. In Spain the chief administrative center under the Moors was called the *Tamarit.* The word *divan* applies to the council held there by the Moorish governors; but *divan* also means a collection or anthology of poems. The particular poems of Lorca's *Divan* are divided among *gacelas* and *casidas,* forms invented by Hafiz, the fourteenth-century Persian poet. These are generally short rhymed verses, mixing religious mysticism with eroticism and episodes of everyday life. In a freer manner, Lorca's poems give such subjects a new ardor and imagery drawn from his own reinvented ballad styles. What emerges is a heightened identification with a restless nature always in conflict and perpetually reflecting an inner landscape of desire, unconsummated passion.

The implicit action of the poems celebrating Granada, the area and arena of his *patria chica* ("The Kingdom of Granada," as he once replied to someone's idle question, "Where are you from?") is that of rediscovery and the sense of homecoming, in which personal memories are tied to the land and culture of Andalusia. The Tamarit, which was also the name of his parents' home in the Huerta de San Vicente, on the outskirts of Granada, was where he returned, for the last time, from Madrid in June 1936, on the eve of the Franco rebellion and where he was senselessly executed on August 19, with all those Spaniards believed infected with the slightest symptoms of liberal-mindedness.

So the *Divan* marks the end of a circle Lorca had made several times, starting when he first left Granada in 1918 and came to live at the Residencia de Estudiantes, the intellectual-and-artist-colony college in Madrid. And then, after the success of his *Gypsy Ballads* in 1928, on being envied and accused of opportunism in using the Gypsy as a subject, Lorca turned away from Spain and everything that had nurtured him there, to encounter a new savage imagery in the cosmopolitan jungle of New York. Living in the city for a year, an Old World savage himself, ignorant of the native language, he even ended up with others one night under the Brooklyn Bridge in the apartment of Hart Crane, soon himself to leave for Mexico and the Caribbean on a last broken journey out of New York.

Beginning in this way to fulfill his own life's mythological round, Lorca searched the New World for a different set of rhythms, metaphors, and people (actually walking the city streets the day of the catastrophic market crash, with suicides leaping from skyscraper windows) to write *Poet in New York.* Then after a brief respite in Cuba, where the Hispanic world began to reorganize itself for him, Lorca returned to Madrid for his last six years, to write the now world-famous dramas *(Blood Wedding, Yerma, Doña Rosita the Spinster,* and *The House of Bernarda Alba)* before going back home finally to die near the Tamarit where he had so often witnessed quiet deaths among the orchards and fountains, the gypsies and the children drowned in the wells. His circle came to a close once and for all, like the dancing bull momentarily outwitting the bullfighter before spilling his own blood communally with the blood of others—bulls and fighters together, just as in the ring a few years before, his friend Ignacio Sánchez Mejías went down, gored on the horns of the bull who went down too.

It may be said that because Lorca had so little time to put together a substantial body of work, much of what he did had to be incomplete—two steps forward, one step back. This staggered progress may also account for the apparent repetitions from one work to another, interrupted by breakthroughs and the leaps ahead to a new style, even where an earlier style predominates. Consequently, a close relationship exists between the farces and the comedies—between, say, *Don*

Perlimplín and *The Shoemaker's Prodigious Wife* where, as with members of the same family, similar facial features, characters, names, even life situations, are shared. *Don Perlimplín,* though a complete one-act play, rooted in the farces, is a complex masterpiece totally different in effect from any of them. And though *Perlimplín* and *Shoemaker* are everywhere different from one another, both plays, having actors and not puppets, are characteristically and motivationally more developed than any of the farces.

The same character types reappear and reassemble themselves in a new, completed action. In the play *When Five Years Pass,* zany and puppet-like features are inherent in the compulsive, often gratuitous behavior of the supporting actors that leads to the main actor's death. In *Play without a Title,* character and action are redirected in political terms, and though incomplete the play might well pass as a farce that turns in on itself. Indeterminacy is the keynote and vital force throughout, as conveyed by the Director within the theatre, exhorting the audience to face reality outside, where a revolution has broken out. Abstract and terrifying in prospect, the menace of the revolution tyrannizes the human characters just as the bully with the billy club, Don Cristóbal, does the puppets in the farces.

It would then seem that the farces and the dialogues are propelled by clockwise and counter-clockwise movements, making for a dynamic of fatalistic action that connects them to the major plays *(Yerma, Blood Wedding, Bernarda Alba)* and to the major poetry as well *(Gypsy Ballads, Poet in New York, Lament for Ignacio Sánchez Mejías)*. Viewed in this light, the farces span the poet's earliest ludic exercises in entertaining the family at home with puppet plays and the poet fifteen years later, who with his teacher, Manuel de Falla, discovered *cante jondo,* folk speech, and a new poetry for the theatre. In the short time he had, the playwright-poet learned how to transfigure the forms that lay close at hand.

"You are the mainstay of the theatre," Lorca told the puppet Cristóbal in the prologue to the Buenos Aires production of the *Tragicomedy of Don Cristóbal and Mistress Rosita* (1934)—"all theatre starts with you," son of Shakespeare's Falstaff.

He was not boasting but stating the facts with playful irony, edged with the pride of a discoverer.

E.H.

FOUR PUPPET PLAYS

The Girl Who Waters the Basil and the Inquisitive Prince

(An Andalusian Tale in Three Engravings and One Color Print)

CAST

Black	Girl	Wise Man 1
Shoemaker	Prince	Wise Man 2
Page	Magician	Wise Man 3

FIRST ENGRAVING

[Street]

BLACK: *(coming from a distance)* I sell stories, I sell tales! I'll sell you a story.... Once upon a time ... once upon a time there was a poor Shoemaker, terribly poor, terribly terribly poor!

SHOEMAKER: *(singing)* Shoemaker, aker, aker,
         stick the awl into the hole!

BLACK: He lived right across from the palace of a rich Prince, a terribly rich, terribly terribly rich Prince.... Prince, sir: would you mind coming out? ... We are doing the introductions!

(Three knocks are heard)

PAGE: His Highness the Prince begs your pardon, but he cannot come out because he is making peepee.

SHOEMAKER AND BLACK: Ahem, ahem, Shoemaker, aker, aker,
         stick the awl into the hole!

BLACK: We ought to explain that the Shoemaker sings with more gusto than anyone.

SHOEMAKER: Ah, my wife was the one who *really* could sing!

BLACK: We ought to explain that the Shoemaker is a widower.

SHOEMAKER: Going on four years.

BLACK: Come, Don Gaiferos, don't keep opening your little box of sad memories!

SHOEMAKER: Well, they've got to know that my name is Don Gaiferos.

BLACK: We ought to explain that the Shoemaker has a daughter.

SHOEMAKER: And her name is Irene Girly-Girl. Step lively, girl!

BLACK: Irene, girl! Are you coming out? Irene! *(turning to the spectators)* Children! Shall we all call her?

ALL: I-reen! I-reen!

IRENE: My eyes they are blue
    and my little heart's as bright
    as a flame of light.

BLACK: The introductions have now been made: the Shoemaker and his daughter Irene. And though our Prince couldn't come out because he was making peepee, he too is introduced.... And now here comes the big thing.... A bright sunny morning, at the hour when a cock crowed and another cock crowed and another and another...quite early, quite a bit early, the Girly-Girl came out to water her basil plant and the very same moment His Highness the Prince came out to take in the cool morning air.

(The GIRL appears at the window and waters the basil plant. The PRINCE also looks out of the Palace window.)

IRENE: *(singing)* Doing the vito, vito, vito,
    doing the vito, vito, *vee*,
    I don't want a soul to see me
    because that makes me blushy.

PRINCE: Girl who waters the plant,
    how many leaves does your basil have?

IRENE: Tell me, you nosy king,
    how many stars has the sky?

(The GIRL shuts her window, and the PRINCE is left there forlorn.)

PRINCE: How many stars has the sky? How many...how many stars?... *(calling out)* Page, page, Mr. Page, come here!

PAGE: You called for me, your Highness the Prince?

PRINCE: Hear me, Page. The Girly-Girl has asked me how many stars has the sky and I didn't know how to reply!

PAGE: How many stars has the sky...? Well, I don't know!

PRINCE: What can I do? I have been made fun of! Page, what can I do?

PAGE: What you can do, Your Highness the Prince, is disguise yourself as a peddler of grapes.

PRINCE: A peddler of grapes?

PAGE: Yes, because that way you'd be able to talk with the Girly-Girl.

PRINCE: Good! Very good! That's what I'll do! *(he leaves)*

PRINCE: *(comes in disguised as a peddler of grapes)*

6

Grapes, little grapes!
I swap little grapes for kisses
with dark-haired little misses.

IRENE: Just how do you swap grapes for kisses?

PRINCE: A little bunch, a little kiss. Another bunch, another kiss.

IRENE: Give me two, one for my father, who drools over them, and another for me.

PRINCE: Two little bunches . . . two little kisses! *(The* PRINCE *gives her two bunches of grapes, and the* GIRL *gives him two kisses)* Adiós, Girl! Adiós *(he goes off singing)* Grapes, fine little grapes!

BLACK: . . . The next day, at the hour when one cock crows and then another cock crows and another and another, Girly-Girl went to the window to water the basil and at the very same moment His Highness the Prince came out for a sniff of the morning breeze. *(He leaves)*

PRINCE: Oh, here comes the girl who waters the basil.

IRENE: *(singing)* With the vito, vito, vito,
with the vito, vito vee.

PRINCE: Girly-Girl! Girly-Girl!
you who water the plant,
how many leaves does your basil have?

IRENE: My nosy Prince,
how many stars has the sky?

PRINCE: Girly-Girl . . .
the kisses you gave the peddler of grapes.

IRENE: Booohooooohooo! *(She goes off crying comically)*

BLACK: . . . Next morning at the hour when one cock crowed and then another cock crowed and another and another. ., our Highness the Prince went to his window. *(He leaves)*

PRINCE: Girly-Girl, you who water the plant,
how many leaves does your basil have?
Won't you come out, girl?

SHOEMAKER: The Girl won't come out because she's insulted by what the grape peddler said.

PRINCE: She won't come out? Why am I wounded by love?
Wounded by love, wounded.
Wounded and dying of love.

BLACK: And so, our Prince His Highness grew sick with melancholy. *(He leaves)*

PRINCE: Ah, from love I come wounded so badly, badly,
  wounded by love, wounded,
  wounded and dying of love!

PAGE: Don't let it worry you, your Highness the Prince. *(crying comically)*

PRINCE: *(who also cries comically)*: O what a burden it is
  to love you as I love you!
  For love of you I am hurt
  by the air, my heart, and my hat!

(slow curtain)

SECOND ENGRAVING

A Hall in the Palace

BLACK: I sell stories! . . . I sell stories! . . . I sell stories! . . . His Highness our Prince fell sick in love for the girl Irene. And I called for a meeting of Wise Men to consult with them. *(he leaves)*

WISE MAN 1: It grows worse every day.

WISE MAN 2: He looks like he's got the Black Pain! He's dying on us, dying of melancholy.

WISE MAN 3: A great magician just arrived in our kingdom with a hat full of stars, and a cure for the sickness of love.

WISE MAN 2: He should be able to cure His Highness our Prince!

WISE MAN 1: Let us summon him to the Palace!

(slow curtain)

THIRD ENGRAVING

Courtyard in the Palace

MAGICIAN: *(It is the girl Irene who comes disguised as a* MAGICIAN *in a black cloak and a hat in the shape of a cone bordered with silver stars and a big cape. On the stage is the tree of the sun and the tree of the moon.)*

I come with a cure for the sickness of love and other magical potions!... Those made ill by melancholy and the moon, come to me! I am the magician of happiness, for I carry the trumpet of laughter!

PRINCE: Magician, Magician, will you be able to cure me?

MAGICIAN: By laurel branches and by the ribbon of Saint Agnes, may your illness be cured and disappear down the little black well of pain!... And so that you're cured of everything totally, get married to Girly-Girl!

PRINCE: With Girly-Girl?

MAGICIAN: Yes, with Irene. *(She takes off her mask)*

PRINCE: Irene! Then will come honey and moons!

MAGICIAN: O my inquisitive Prince!

PRINCE: Irene! Irene!

IRENE: ... Irene! ... García.

PRINCE: Oh Irene! You'd really like to marry me?

IRENE: Yes, my inquisitive Prince!

PRINCE: From now on we shall live with the imp of joy in our hearts!

PRINCE AND IRENE: *(singing together)*
Girl, girl, who waters the basil,
how many leaves has your plant?

IRENE: Will you show me each morning the little cock that sings about everything?

PRINCE: And I'll teach you where the heart's tiny imp dwells.

IRENE: Ohhhhhh!

PRINCE: Yes, he dwells under the pillow of the child who is pure.

IRENE: Pure?

PRINCE: Yes, pure as the wild things that grow in the salad days of the soul!

PRINCE AND IRENE: Girl, girl, who waters your plant,
how many leaves does your basil have?
Girl, girl, you who water your plant,
how many leaves does it have?

(The actors all leave singing rounds. One can't tell if the sun or the moon shines more bright. The curtain falls slowly.)

9

Cristobical

Tomfoolery

CAST

Old Man with a Guitar
Blind Man's Helper
Currito
The Girls
The Boys
Distant Voices

Uncle Who Plays the
    Carrañacas
Gypsy
Blind Man With the Guitar
Doña Rosita
Don Woodsman-Heart

Cristóbal

SCENE I

Painted on the backdrop, an Andalusian town with melancholy arcades. In the background, a big mountain in deep ochre, crowned by a blue-blackness where stars of live gold shine. At right and left, two yellow palm trees.

It is the morning of the fiesta of Saint John in an Andalusian town. A group of girls are awaiting the stroke of midnight to wash their faces in be-witched water.

OLD MAN WITH A GUITAR: *(sings)* Yellow flower,
                                        everyday
                                        flower.

BLIND MAN'S HELPER: Old Sol of a snail,
                              col col,
                              caracol pink.

CURRITO: *(in a blue suit, flat little hat and cape, sings)*
        We sally forth
        at break of day
        in a petal of yours,
        everyday
        flower.

THE GIRLS: Oh the morn of Saint John,
                  oh, chilly morning.

THE BOYS: Oh, the morn of my love
                 on the road to Seville.

CURRITO: When will you open your window,
                Doña Rosita?
                Before
                the flower of yellow
                bursts open?

BLIND MAN WITH GUITAR: Everyday
              flower.

BLIND MAN'S HELPER: Old Sol of a snail,
              col col,
              caracol pink.

CURRITO: At midnight
              you'll wash
              in a stream of clear water.
              Oh let the drops get lost
              in your blouse!

THE GIRLS: The River Guadalquivir
              has a hidden star.
              My love is searching for it
              up the Guadalquivir.

THE BOYS: Down the Guadalquivir.

THE GIRLS: Up the Guadalquivir.

UNCLE WHO PLAYS THE CARRAÑACAS: To the carrañaca, ñaca,
              the carrañaca of girls
              without love, without windows.

GYPSY: *(motionless)* Ah, moon, moon, dear little moon.

CURRITO: Girls, to the clear water!

THE GIRLS: Crystalline water,
              there where the precious
              cinnamon bloom
              is first born.

(One by one there emerge the twelve hours of midnight. They are women dressed in black mohair, the style of mid-nineteenth century: bustle, long train with ruffles, and a calañes hat with chin strap. They carry enormous brown fans. They are copper-colored brunettes.)

SCENE II

Dance of the twelve midnight hours.

They will move slowly, opening their fans till they place them in the form of a peacock's tail on their bustles.

BLIND MAN WITH GUITAR: The traveller draws away.
　　　　　　　　　　Oil lamps are snuffed out.
　　　　　　　　　　Ah, bloodless heart!

DOÑA ROSITA: *(offstage)* Through the air,
　　　　　　　through the air...

BLIND MAN WITH GUITAR: The four corners of Cádiz
　　　　　　　　　　are all deserted.
　　　　　　　　　　In Granada the water
　　　　　　　　　　has fallen asleep.
　　　　　　　　　　Ah, bloodless heart!

DOÑA ROSITA: *(offstage)* The sighs of my love
　　　　　　　pass through the air.

(The twelve hours emerge slowly closing their fans. The other characters follow, except for CURRITO and the BLIND MAN.)

BLINDMAN WITH GUITAR: Throw a lemon
　　　　　　　　　from above!

EVERYBODY ELSE: *(offstage)* A lemon...

INTERMEZZO

A forest in the spring; flowers extend to the tree-tops. On the left is a cabin shaped like a heart facing downward; DON WOODSMAN-HEART *lives inside. He is a little stooped-over man, dressed in red, his head crowned with poppies. Before him the light of a campfire burns among the roses.*

DISTANT VOICES: Whoever invents an engine
　　　　　　　to measure love by
　　　　　　　will find very few
　　　　　　　who have a heart.

DON WOODSMAN-HEART: Those simple folk are right! There are men who have a tree inside of them, others an eye, others a mouth. Nothing but a mouth! But a heart! Ha, ha, ha. There is even someone who's full of sawdust! Cork dust! Ha, ha, ha.

DISTANT VOICES: Earth is a crossroads,
　　　　　　　and the roads all gray!
　　　　　　　Earth is a crossroads,
　　　　　　　is what the fir trees say.

DON WOODSMAN-HEART: I know it only too well! I should have burned down my cabin long ago.... But they tell me, "Little old man, you're still useful: at least you can still clear the woods of poisonous plants."

DISTANT VOICES: Col col, old Sol of a snail,
on the breast of my love!
Moon, moon, little old moon,
in the eyes of my girl!

DON WOODSMAN-HEART: The roots of trees disturb me and the tiny lights that wink in the night. The symphony of insects disturbs me and the life of corollas.

CRISTÓBAL: *(from the right)* Caramba! I can barely manage to creep around! Ay, I can't go on like this! Ay, if I could only grin and bear it! Caramba! *(wobbling)* Caramba!

DON WOODSMAN-HEART: What are you doing here, old Billy-Club man?

CRISTÓBAL: I already know you don't want my silver or my gold, but I have taken out my billy-club and—damn!—it's been broken!

DON WOODSMAN-HEART: Get along with you!

CRISTÓBAL: I am getting married tomorrow and my limbs are growing heavy. This wheel, above all, doesn't work and my director told me, "See to it that that man winds you up, you know?" And that's why I've come.

DON WOODSMAN-HEART: For the last time, come over here, do you hear?

CRISTÓBAL: For the last time!

(The WOODSMAN *winds up* CRISTÓBAL.*)*

DISTANT VOICES: Wind through the hills.
The wind passes
over the sea, over the plain
and the sky.

CRISTÓBAL: I'm all right! *(exasperated)* But hurry, it's getting late now! The hour draws near when I must get dressed. Goodbye! What the devil! No one will be able to tell anything about me! Caramba! Goodbye, goodbye! *(he leaves)*

(The WOODSMAN *stirs up his fire)*
(Music)

16

In The Frame of Don Cristóbal:
A Puppet Farce

CAST

Poet	Invalid
Director	Mother
Cristóbal	Frank
	Rosita

PROLOGUE

Ladies and Gentlemen:

The poet who has interpreted and adapted this puppet farce from the lips of the people has evidence of the fact that the distinguished audience this afternoon will be able to appreciate with intelligence and good nature the deliciously crude language of the puppets.

Every popular puppet show has the same rhythm, the same fantasy and the same enchanting sense of freedom which the poet has here preserved in the dialogue.

The puppet show is the expression of the people's imagination, offering the temperature of its grace and innocence.

The poet knows that the audience will hear with joy and simplicity the expressions and words born of the earth; and that these will serve as purifiers, now, when vulgarities, falsehoods, and strained feelings reach deepest into the home.

(Enter the Poet.)

POET: Men and women, attention! Child, be still! I want you to be so quiet, so profoundly still, that we shall be able to hear the glu-glu of the grasshoppers. And if a bird should move its wing, let us also hear it; and if a little ant should move its foot, let us also hear it; and if a heart should beat strongly, let it seem like a hand dividing the weeds at the shore. Ay! Ay! It will be necessary for the young ladies to close their fans and for the girls to take off their silken kerchiefs, so that we may hear and see all this business about Rosita, married to Cristóbal, and all this business about Cristóbal, married to Rosita.

Ay! Ay! They are beating the drum. Weep or you laugh—it doesn't matter to me in the least what you do. I'm going to eat a little bread now, the tiniest of bread crusts the birds have left me; and then I'm going to press the costumes of the company.

(Looks around to see if he is being observed)
I want to tell you that I know how roses are born and how the stars grew out of the sea, but . . .

DIRECTOR: Please favor us with keeping still! The prologue ends where you say, "I'm going to press the costumes of the company."

POET: Yes, sir.

DIRECTOR: As a poet you have no business prying into the secrets in which we all live.

POET: Yes, sir.

DIRECTOR: Don't I pay you a decent salary?

POET: Yes, sir; but I want to say that I know that at heart Cristóbal is good, and perhaps could be so.

DIRECTOR: Loud-mouth! If you don't shut up, I'll break your cornbread crust in half. Who are you to determine the laws of good and evil?

POET: I'm finished; I'll be still.

DIRECTOR: No sir! Say what you're expected to say, and what the audience knows to be true.

POET: Honorable people: as a poet I'm obliged to inform you that Cristóbal is bad.

DIRECTOR: And he cannot be good.

POET: And he cannot be good.

DIRECTOR: All right, let's go now.

POET: I'm coming, Mr. Director. And he never can be any good.

DIRECTOR: Very well. Now, how much do I owe you?

POET: Five bucks!

DIRECTOR: Here you are.

POET: No! I don't want it in gold. Gold is like fire, and I'm a poet of the night. Give it to me in silver. Silver coins will be lit up by the moon.

DIRECTOR: Ha, ha! So much the better for me. Now, to begin.

POET: Open your balcony, Rosita.
The show is about to begin.
A dead old woman's waiting,
And a sleepy-headed husband.

DIRECTOR: Cristóbal!

CRISTÓBAL: What?

DIRECTOR: Please enter. The audience is waiting.

CRISTÓBAL: I'm coming.

DIRECTOR: And Rosita?

ROSITA: I'm putting my shoes on.
  (*Snores are heard.*)

DIRECTOR: What's that? Is Cristóbal snoring already?

CRISTÓBAL: I'm coming, Mr. Director. I've just finished pissing.

DIRECTOR: Quiet! And don't be so vulgar!

CRISTÓBAL (*appearing*): Good evening, gentlemen.

DIRECTOR: Hurry, Cristóbal; the play must go on. That is your cue. You're a doctor.

CRISTÓBAL: I'm a doctor. All right, let's get to the point.

DIRECTOR: Remember, Cristóbal. You need money to get married.

CRISTÓBAL: Yes, of course.

DIRECTOR: Well, earn it then, right away.

CRISTÓBAL: Let me get my club.

DIRECTOR: Bravo. I see you understand me perfectly.

INVALID: Good day.

CRISTÓBAL: Good night.

INVALID: Good afternoon.

CRISTÓBAL: And a black good night.

INVALID (*timidly*): It could be good night, maybe.

CRISTÓBAL: A shut up good night.

INVALID: In view of what you say, I am convinced that you're a great doctor and that you'll be able to cure me. (*energetically*) Good day.

CRISTÓBAL: I said, good night and good night it is!

INVALID: Bravo. As you say.

CRISTÓBAL: Now, what ails you?

INVALID: My neck is sick
where the hair grows thick.
It wasn't such a wreck
Till I was told by my heck
of a cousin, John Neck.

CRISTÓBAL: This will end with your being de-necked.

(Seizes him)

INVALID: Ay! ay! ay! ay! Cristóbal!

CRISTÓBAL: Come on. Be good enough to stretch your neck a little so I can regulate the carotid.

INVALID: Ay! I can't move it.

CRISTÓBAL: I tell you: try moving the carotid.

INVALID: Ay! it's impossible.

CRISTÓBAL: Open the jugular vein yourself, with your hands.

INVALID: If I could, I would have done so already. *(aggressively)* Good day, good day, good day, day.

CRISTÓBAL: Now you'll see day.

(Leaves. The INVALID *groans, stretched out on the railing.)*

INVALID: Ay! Ay! How my carotid aches! Ay! My carotid. I have carotiditis.

CRISTÓBAL *(returning with a club):* Here I am.

INVALID: And what's that, Cristóbal?

CRISTÓBAL: A stick to mix the liquor pot.

INVALID: How are you going to use it?

CRISTÓBAL: To make your neck hot.

INVALID: Please, I don't want a licking.

CRISTÓBAL: Nothing lost in a little sticking.
Have you much money?

INVALID: Twenty bucks, twenty bucks, twenty.
And under my vest aplenty,
six bucks, three bucks, three.
And if you'll spy in my ass's little eye,
you'll see another little roll of twenty.

CRISTÓBAL: Well, now I'm going to cure you.
And you won't have much to pay.

INVALID (*aggressive*): Good day, good day, good day, good day, good day, good day.

CRISTÓBAL (*hitting him with the club*): Good night. I'll show you. Stick your neck out.

INVALID: I can't, Cristóbal.

CRISTÓBAL (*beating him*): Stick your neck out!

INVALID: Ay! My carotid.

CRISTÓBAL: More neck.

INVALID: Ay! My carotid.

CRISTÓBAL: More neck! (*a blow*) More neck, more neck, more neck!!

(*The* INVALID *extends his neck a yard.*)

INVALID: Ayyyyyyyy!

(*The* INVALID *extends his neck full-length and rises, but* CRISTÓBAL *gives him the final death blow.*)

CRISTÓBAL: There, you're a goner today,
        One, two and three.
        Over the cliff with him.

(*A loud thud is heard.*)

        Hurray, hurray, hurray, hurray!

DIRECTOR: Did he have any money?

CRISTÓBAL: Yes.

DIRECTOR: Well, now for holy matrimony.

CRISTÓBAL: For holy matrimony.

DIRECTOR: Here comes Rosita's mother. You must speak with her.

MOTHER: I'm the mother of Rosita
        and I want her wed.
        For her breasts, now they seem,
        like two tangerines,
        and her little ass round
        like cheese by the pound,
        and her birdie between
        can sing and can scream.
        As I tell you, make ready:
        Rosita needs a hubby,
        and if possible, two.
        Ha! Ha! Ha! Ha!

CRISTÓBAL: Lady!

MOTHER: Sir, sir, sir, sir,
       Sir pen and ink-stirrer.

CRISTÓBAL: I don't wear a cap of fur.
       But as you said,
       I want to be wed.

MOTHER: I have a daughter.
       How much will you give?

CRISTÓBAL: An ounce of pure gold
       from an Arab's ass rolled;
       an ounce of pure silver
       the cat's ass will deliver;
       and some of the baptismal coin
       her mother spent to make her Christian.

MOTHER: And also: I want a mule to ride on
       to see the moon rise in Lisbon.

CRISTÓBAL: A mule's too much; I stop there, woman.

MOTHER: You have silver, Mr. Cristóbal.
       Now, Rosita's young and you're old.
       Old, old, and your knees all bowed.

CRISTÓBAL: And you're the haggard old crone,
       wipes her ass with a paving stone.

MOTHER: Drunkard! Dirty sot!

CRISTÓBAL: I'm going to keep your belly hot.
       You can count on the mule. Where's Rosita?

MOTHER: Fixing her chemise in her dressing room.
       And she's there all alone.
       Ha! Ha! Ha!

CRISTÓBAL: Ay! Now I'm getting a bone!

MOTHER: Ay! And dancing all alone!
       Ay! And dancing all alone!

CRISTÓBAL: I want her photo to judge her appeal.

MOTHER: But first, let us seal the deal.

CRISTÓBAL: Rosita, I want to see
       the soles of your feet,

to see if they please me,
the soles of your feet.

MOTHER: O, her feet you'll see
when the two of you play.
If you give me the money
I'll do what you say.

(Leaves singing.)

(Music)

VOICE OF ROSITA: Dancing the vito, I moan,
with the vito I'll slowly expire;
each hour, my boy, my own,
drawn closer to your fire.

(ROSITA enters)

ROSITA: Ay! A night so bright and clear
breathes over the tiles.
The hour when boys
count the stars
and old dotards
nod under their horses,
while I yearn to be:
lying with John
on the diván,
on the mattress to lay
with beautiful Ray,
upon a settee
with Joey,
on the seat
with Pete,
on the floor
with the one I care for,
stuck to the door
with handsome Arthur,
on the roomy chaise lounge
with Ray, Pete and John,
with Arthur and Joey.
Ay! ay! ay! ay! ay!
I want to be wed; anybody hear me?
I want to be wed
to some young fop,

to a young guard,
to an archbishop,
to some general,
to someone playful and bold
who knows how to hold,
to twenty young fellows
from Portugal.

CRISTÓBAL: All right. Agreed?

MOTHER: Agreed!

CRISTÓBAL: Of course, if you say no, I can show you my club, and you know what would happen then!

MOTHER: Ay! What have I done?

CRISTÓBAL: Afraid?

MOTHER (trembling): Ay!

CRISTÓBAL: Say it: "I'm afraid."

MOTHER: I'm afraid.

CRISTÓBAL: Say: "Cristóbal is my master."

MOTHER: Cristóbal is my master.

CRISTÓBAL: As I shall be your daughter's master too.

MOTHER: Then . . .

CRISTÓBAL: I give you the ounce of gold from an Arab's ass rolled, and you'll hand over your daughter, Rosita, thanking me the while since she's just ripe and ready for plucking.

MOTHER: She's twenty years old.

CRISTÓBAL: I say that she's ripe, and so be it. But above all, she's a beautiful wench. Say it, say it, say it.

MOTHER: Her two little titties, now they seem,
like two tangerines,
and her little ass round
like cheese by the pound;
and her birdie between . . .

CRISTÓBAL: Ayyyyyyyyy!

MOTHER: . . . and her birdie between
can sing and can scream.

CRISTÓBAL: Yes, sir. I'm going to be married because Rosita is a *boccato di cardinale*.

26

MOTHER: Does Your Honor speak Italian?

CRISTÓBAL: No. But in my youth, I went through France and Italy lackeying to a certain Mr. Trousers. But that or anything else about my life is no business of yours. Tremble! Everything behind me must tremble, you old witch, must tremble!

MOTHER: I'm trembling already!

CRISTÓBAL: Call Rosita.

MOTHER: Rositaaaaaaaaa!

ROSITA: What do you want?
    I want to be married
    to a premature calf,
    to a crocodile,
    to a mule,
    to an army general.
    As long as it's a he,
    it's all the same to me.

CRISTÓBAL: Ay! What lovely little hams she has, before and behind!

MOTHER: Do you want to be married?

ROSITA: I want to be married.

MOTHER: Do you want to be married?

CRISTÓBAL: I want to be married.

MOTHER (weeping): O, don't beat her, sir, please! Ay! What a crying shame for my child!

CRISTÓBAL: Call the priest!

(The MOTHER goes out screaming. CRISTÓBAL joins ROSITA and together they go off to church. Bells ring.)

POET: Have you seen it all? Well, maybe it's better to have a good laugh over it. The moon is a white eagle. The moon is a hen laying eggs. For the poor, the moon is a loaf of bread, and for the rich, a tambourine with white, stretched hide. But Rosita and Cristóbal do not see the moon. If the director of the play is willing, Cristóbal will see water nymphs, and Rosita will be able to fill his hair with icicles in the third act when snow begins to fall on all the innocents. But the owner of this theatre has all the players shut up in a tiny iron cage, so only ladies with silk bosoms and ridiculous noses may see them, and only gentlemen with beards who go to their clubs saying: Ca-ram-ba! Really, Cristóbal is not like this at all, nor is Rosita.

DIRECTOR: Who's prattling there?

POET: I was just saying they are resting.

DIRECTOR: Be kind enough not to stick your nose into it. If I had imagination, I'd have thrown you into the gutter long ago.

CRISTÓBAL: Ay! Rosita.

ROSITA: Have you drunk too much?

CRISTÓBAL: If I were made of wine I could drink myself all up. Haaa! And my belly a big pie, a big pie with plums and yams. Rosita, sing something for me.

ROSITA: I shall.

(sings)

What do you want me to sing? The can-can by Goichoechea or the Marseillaise by Gil Robles? Ay! Cristóbal! I'm frightened. What are you going to do to me?

CRISTÓBAL: I shall do you muuuuuuuuuuuuuu.

ROSITA: Ay! Don't put me in such a fright!
What will you do to me at midnight?

CRISTÓBAL: I shall do you aaaaaaaaaaaaaaaaaa.

ROSITA: Ay! Don't give me such a shock!
What will you do to me at three o'clock?

CRISTÓBAL: I shall do you piiiiiiiiiiiiiiiiiii.

ROSITA: Then you will see
my birdie fly.

(They embrace.)

CRISTÓBAL: Ay, Rosita mine.

ROSITA: Have you had too much booze?
Why not take a snooze?

CRISTÓBAL: I am going to sleep in my cups
to see if my linnet wakens me up.

ROSITA: Yes, yes, yes, yes, yes.

(CRISTÓBAL *snores.* FRANK *enters and embraces* ROSITA *and loud kisses are heard.*)

CRISTÓBAL *(awakening):* What was that, Rosita?

ROSITA: Ay, ay, ay! Don't you see how big the moon is? How it shimmers, how it shiiiiiiiiines? It's my shadow. Shadow, go away!

CRISTÓBAL: Go away, shadow.

ROSITA: How troublesome the moon is, Cristóbal. No? Why don't you take another little snooze?

CRISTÓBAL: I'll take another little rest
to see if my dove stirs from its nest.

ROSITA: Ya, ya, ya, ya, ya, ya.

(The POET enters, begins to kiss ROSITA, and CRISTÓBAL awakens.)

CRISTÓBAL: What was that, Rosita?

ROSITA: Don't you see how the moonlight wanes? It is...it is...the machine that runs the bobbin thread for making lace. Don't you hear how it sounds?

(Kisses are heard.)

CRISTÓBAL: Seems to sound too much.

ROSITA: Go away then, machine.
You are right, Cristobita.
Why not take another snooze?

CRISTÓBAL: I'll take another little rest
to see if my dove can sleep in its nest.

(The INVALID enters from the other side and ROSITA kisses him too.)

CRISTÓBAL: What was that I heard?

ROSITA: It's the beginning of sundown.

CRISTÓBAL: Brrr. What's that? Was that you?

ROSITA: Don't get so upset. It's the frogs in the pond.

CRISTÓBAL: So they are. This story will end and will never end. Brrrrr.

ROSITA: But don't cry out like that. It's the lions in the circus, it's the jilted husbands shouting in the streets.

MOTHER: Rositaaaaaaa. The doctor is here.

ROSITA: Ay! The doctor. Ay! ay! ay! ay! My belly.

MOTHER: Evil man, dog. All because of you, because of you, we must give all your money away.

ROSITA: All your money. Ay ay! ay!

(They go out.)

DIRECTOR: Cristóbal.

CRISTÓBAL: What's going on?

DIRECTOR: Hurry down, immediately; Rosita is ill.

CRISTÓBAL: What's the matter with her?

DIRECTOR: She's giving birth.

CRISTÓBAL: Birrrrrrrrrrrrrrrrrth?

DIRECTOR: She has had four children.

CRISTÓBAL: Ay, Rosita. So this is how you pay me off! Little whore! And the hundred dollars you cost me. Pin, pan, brrrr.

(ROSITA is screaming behind the scene.)

CRISTÓBAL: Whose children are they?

MOTHER: Yours, yours, yours.

CRISTÓBAL *(slaps her):* Whose children are they?

MOTHER: Yours, yours, yours.

(CRISTÓBAL slaps her again. ROSITA, giving birth, is screaming.)

DIRECTOR: Now the fifth one is being born.

CRISTÓBAL: Whose is the fifth one?

MOTHER: Yours.

(CRISTÓBAL beats her.)

CRISTÓBAL: Whose is it?

MOTHER: Yours, yours, yours, and only yours.

(Beats her.)

Yours, yours, yours, yours.

(Dies and lies still, bent over the railing.)

CRISTÓBAL: You're a goner, old bitch, you're a goner. Now I'll know whose children they are.

(He goes out.)

MOTHER *(getting up):* Yours, yours, yours, yours.

(CRISTÓBAL returns to beat her, entering and leaving with ROSITA.)

CRISTÓBAL: Take that, and that, and that . . .

(The DIRECTOR *enters with his large head sticking out of the set.)*

DIRECTOR: Enough!

(He grabs the puppets and holds them up to the audience.)

Ladies and Gentlemen:

The Andalusian people have often listened to such comedies under the gray branches of the olive trees and in the darkened air of abandoned stables. Here, there are the eyes of mules, hard as fists; here, the embroidered leather of Cordoban harnesses; and here, the soft, dewy bunches of the spiked ears of grain; here, with merriment and enchanting innocence, have burst those expressions which we passively endure in city places confused with alcohol and cards. These "dirty" words acquire ingenuity and freshness when spoken by puppets enacting with charm an ancient puppet farce. Let us fill the theatre with fresh ears of grain, where coarse expressions will oppose the tedium and vulgarity of the stage to which we have been condemned. Let us greet today the slap-stick Cristóbal, the Andalusian, cousin of the Galician Bululu, and brother-in-law of Aunt Norica of Cádiz, brother of the Parisian Monsieur Guiñol, and uncle of Harlequin of Bergamo, as one of the characters after whom the good old smell of the theatre purely trails.

Dialogue of the Poet and Don Cristóbal

(Introduction to the performance of The Billy-Club Puppets *by
Federico García Lorca and Manuel Fontanals in Buenos Aires
on March 26, 1934)*

CRISTÓBAL: Ladies and Gentlemen: This is not the first time that I, Don Cristóbal, the drunken puppet who marries Doña Rosita, leaves the hand of Federico García Lorca on the stage, where I live and never die. The first time was in the house of this poet— remember that, Federico? It was spring in Granada, and the drawing room of your house was full of children who were saying: "The puppets are flesh and bone, so how come they remain children and never grow up?" The famous Manuel de Falla was at the piano and there performed for the first time in Spain Stravinsky's *Histoire d'un soldat.* I still remember the smiling faces of the newsboys whom the poet invited in among the curls and ribbons on the heads of the rich children.

I appear again today in Buenos Aires to perform before you and am grateful for the attention given him and Manolo Fontanals. I personally don't much care to perform in these theatres because I don't speak very well. Here it's the painted drops and the moon of the sensible theatre that counts. I'm used to performing among the water reeds at night during the Andalusian summer, surrounded by simple girls given to blushing easily and shepherd boys with prickly beards like pine needles.

But the poet wants to bring me out here.

POET: You are the mainstay of the theatre, Don Cristóbal. All theatre starts with you. There was once a poet in England, called Shakespeare, who created a character called Falstaff, who is your son.

CRISTÓBAL: Well, you'd know him better than I, but I'm not fond of electric lights.

POET: I believe the theatre must return to you.

CRISTÓBAL: The truth is that I am fond of you. This Federico is a mad

man! He's always dragging me out, and though I...to me..,
well, do madcap things, it's to please you.

POET: They do please me. I've loved you since childhood, Cristobita,
and when I'm old I'll still join you to amuse children who have
never been in a theatre.

CRISTÓBAL: I'm getting sad.

POET: What about?

CRISTÓBAL: I'm going off with Lorca and with Fontanals. They tell me
to say goodbye to you first, because first and last I cannot shed
tears and they can...and they don't want to be sad. Thanks to
you all, ladies and gentlemen. Many kisses to the company and to
Lola who always remembers us and you, Federico, who always
loved her.

POET: My thanks to you all, ladies and gentlemen. And now to get to
business. Ay! but do forgive the puppets for not being great ac-
tors because they've been sleeping lo! these many years, forgotten
by everybody. Salud.

THE BILLY-CLUB PUPPETS

Tragicomedy of Don Cristóbal and Mistress Rosita

(A Punch-and-Judy Farce in Six Scenes and a Prologue)

CAST

Mosquito
Rosita
Father
Cocoliche
Coachman
Don Cristobita
Servant
An Hour
Young Men (3)
Smugglers
Espanatanublos (Scareclouds),
   Tavern Keeper

Currito, man from the Harbor
Cansa-Almas (Bore-Stiff),
   Shoemaker
Fígaro, Barber
Urchin
Young Lady in Yellow
Blind Beggar
Maja (with beauty marks)
Acolyte
Wedding Guests with Torches
Funeral Priests
Cortege

PROLOGUE

The sound of trumpets and drums. MOSQUITO will come on from wherever he wishes. MOSQUITO is a mysterious character, half spirit, half goblin, half insect. He enacts the joy of the free life and the grace and poetry of the Andalusian people. He carries a toy trumpet.

MOSQUITO: Men and women! Attention! Shut that little mouth of yours, boy! And you, girl, take a seat and hold your horses. Be quiet and let the silence grow clear as a fountain at home. Let the quiet seep in as the last whispers fade and die. *(drum beats)* My company and I come from the bourgeois theatre, the theatre of dukes and counts, a crystal and gold theatre, where men go to fall asleep, and women as well. My company and I were shut-ins there. You can't imagine how painful that was for us. But one day I saw through the little key hole of some door a star trembling, like a fresh violet of light. I opened my eye wide as I could—the wind's finger kept wanting to close it for me—and under the star a broad river smiled in the furrows of slow boats. Then I told my friends, and we fled into the meadows searching for simple folk to show them things—little things, the tiniest things in the world, under the green moon of the mountains and under the rose moon of the shores. And now that the moon is rising and the glow worms flee slowly away to their little caves, it's time to start the great show called *Tragicomedy of Don Cristóbal and Mistress Rosita*. ...Get ready to bear up under the mean little fist-clouting Don Cristóbal and weep with the sweet little nothings of Mistress Rosita, who more than a woman is a lapwing on a pond, a delicate little lady bird from snow-land. *(He goes off but runs back again.)* And now...for the wind! Fan every astonished face, and bear away every sigh over the top of that mountain range, and dry every tear off the eyes of the girls who have no sweetheart.

My little tree had
four little leaves
beginning to grow—
and the wind shook them so!

FIRST SCENE

A room downstairs in Doña Rosita's house. In the rear, a large
iron window grating and door. Visible through the grating is a
small orchard of orange trees. Rosita is dressed in rose and a bus-
tle covered with laces and bows. As the curtain rises, she sits em-
broidering on a huge frame.

ROSITA: One, two, three, four... *(She sticks herself.)* Ouch! *(Bringing her
finger to her mouth)* That makes four times now I've stuck myself on
this last letter of "To My Adorable Father." Needlepoint embroi-
dery is really hard work. One, two... *(She loosens the needle.)* Oh,
how I'd love to get married! I'll put a yellow flower in my topknot
and a veil that'll go trailing all the way down the street! *(She stands
up.)* And when the barber's daughter looks out of her window, I'll
tell her, "I'm going to be married before you are, way before you,
with bracelets and all." *(Someone whistles outside.)* Uh-oh, that's him,
my boy!

FATHER *(outside):* Rositaaaa!

ROSITA *(taken aback):* Whaaaat! *(Runs back and sits down at the embroidery
frame, blowing kisses to the window.)*

FATHER *(entering):* I just wanted to see if you were at your embroi-
dery.... Keep at it, dearest daughter, because that puts food on
the table. Ah, how short we are of money! Out of the five money
bags inherited from your uncle the bishop, there's not this much
left!

ROSITA: Oh what a great beard my uncle the bishop had! What a
sweetheart he was! *(A whistle outside)* And what a great whistler
too! Really great!

FATHER: But daughter, what are you saying? Are you going crazy?

ROSITA: Well, no, no...! I was mistaken.

FATHER: Ah, Rosita. We're so deep in debt! What's to become of us? *(He takes out his handkerchief and weeps.)*

ROSITA *(weeping):* But...of course...you...I...

FATHER: If at least you wanted to marry, that would be another story; but it seems to me that for the time being...

ROSITA: I *have* been thinking about it.

FATHER: You have?

ROSITA: But hadn't you noticed? How imperceptive men are!

FATHER: Well, you couldn't have picked a better moment, no sir!

ROSITA: I just can't wait to put up my hair, and put some rouge on my cheeks...

FATHER: So you mean you agree?

ROSITA *(pretending a nunlike innocence):* Yes, father.

FATHER: And you won't back out of it?

ROSITA: No, father.

FATHER: And you'll always obey me?

ROSITA: Yes, father.

FATHER: Well, that's all I wanted to know. *(turning to leave)* I've been saved from ruination! I've been saved! *(leaves)*

ROSITA: What can that mean, "I've been saved from ruination! I've been saved!"? Because my sweetheart Cocoliche has less money than we do. Much less! He inherited from his grandma three dollars and a jar of quince jelly, and nothing else! Ah, but I love him, I love him, I love him, and love-love-love him! *(spoken with increasing rapidity)* Let everyone else take money; I'll just take love. *(She runs to the window grating and waves a large rose kerchief through the bars.)*

VOICE OF COCOLICHE *(singing to a guitar):* The sighs of my love
flow through the air,
flow through the air
and away they go.

ROSITA *(singing):* The sighs of my love
flow through the air,
flow through the air
and away they go.

COCOLICHE *(appearing at the window):* Who goes there?

ROSITA *(hiding her face behind a large fan and disguising her voice):* Peaceable folk.

COCOLICHE: Does a certain Rosita live here?

ROSITA: She's taking a bath.

COCOLICHE *(making as if to leave):* Well, may it do her some good.

ROSITA *(revealing herself):* And would you really be capable of going away?

COCOLICHE: I would not. *(sweetly)* By your side my feet turn to lead.

ROSITA: Want to know something?

COCOLICHE: What?

ROSITA: I don't dare.

COCOLICHE: Dare!

ROSITA *(seriously):* Look, I don't want to be a shameless woman.

COCOLICHE: Seems a pretty good idea to me.

ROSITA: Look, it happens that . . .

COCOLICHE: Say it!

ROSITA: I'll hide behind my fan.

COCOLICHE *(desperate):* My dear girl!

ROSITA *(behind the fan):* That I want to marry you.

COCOLICHE: What are you saying?

ROSITA: What you heard!

COCOLICHE: Oh, Rosita!

ROSITA: And right away.

COCOLICHE: Right away I'm going to write to Paris asking for a baby boy . . .

ROSITA: Listen, to Paris? Not on your life, because I don't want him to take after the French, with their chou chou chou.

COCOLICHE: Then . . .

ROSITA: We'll ask for one from Madrid.

COCOLICHE: But does your father know about it?

ROSITA *(lowering her fan):* And he's given me his permission!

COCOLICHE: Ah, my dear Rosita! Come, come! Come closer to me!

ROSITA: But don't start getting nervous!

COCOLICHE: It feels as if I were being tickled on the soles of my feet. Come closer.

ROSITA: No, no. I'll give you my kisses from here. *(They exchange kisses from a distance; noise of bells ringing.)* This always happens. Now someone is coming. Goodbye until tonight!

(Bells are heard ringing and in the big window in the back a carriage appears, drawn by little cardboard horses with panaches of feathers, the carriage stops.)

CRISTOBITA *(from the carriage):* Sure enough, she is the prettiest girl in town.

ROSITA *(curtsying with her skirts):* Thanks very much.

CRISTOBITA: She I'll definitely take. I guess she is almost three feet tall. A woman shouldn't be any taller or shorter. But what a figure, and what bearing! You could almost say she's charmed me. Whip 'em up, driver—get going. *(carriage slowly moves away)*

ROSITA *(mocking):* Now that's a good one! "She I'll definitely take." What an ugly and ill-bred man! He must be one of those half-crazy foreigners. *(A pearl necklace drops through the window.)* God, what's this? Oh, what a darling string of pearls! *(She puts it on and looks at herself in a hand-mirror.)* Genevieve of Brabant could have one like this when she set about waiting for her husband up in the tower of her castle. Ah, and it looks so nice on me . . . But who sent it?

FATHER *(entering):* Oh, my daughter, endless happiness ahead. Arrangements for your wedding are all made!

ROSITA: How grateful I am to you, and Cocoliche will be too. Why, just now . . .

FATHER: What do you mean Cocoliche, and what the heck are you talking about? I've given your hand in marriage to Don Cristobita the Billy-Club man, who just went by here in his carriage.

ROSITA: I don't love him, I don't love him, and that's that! And my hand is mine and can't be taken away from me. I have a sweetheart . . . and I'll throw away this necklace.

FATHER: Well, there's no way out of it. The man has lots of gold and that suits me; otherwise we'll have to go begging in the street tomorrow.

ROSITA: Then we'll beg.

FATHER: I'm in charge here because I'm the father. It's all been said and done, the kettle's on the fire! There's nothing more to be said.

ROSITA: It's just that...

FATHER: Be quiet.

ROSITA: But I...

FATHER: That's *it!* *(Exit)*

ROSITA: Oh me oh my! Well, I'll say—he disposes of my hand and I've got to stand for it because that's what the law says. *(weeps)* Why shouldn't the law stay where it belongs and mind its own business. If I could only sell my soul to the devil. *(shouting)* Come out, Come out, come out here, devil, because I don't want to marry Cristóbal at all!

FATHER *(entering):* What's all this hullaballoo! Back to your needlework and be quiet. What times we live in! Will children tell parents what to do? You're going to follow every one of my wishes just as I followed my father's when he married me to your mother, who, by the way, had such a moonface that... that...

ROSITA: All right, I won't say another word!

FATHER *(as he leaves):* Have you ever seen the likes of it?

ROSITA: Very well, then. Between our fathers and the priests, we girls have had it up to here! *(sits down to embroider)* Every afternoon— three, four—the parish priest tells us: you're heading straight for hell! You'll be scorched to death! Worse than dogs!... but I say that dogs get hitched with anyone they want and they have such a wonderful time of it! How I'd love to be a dog! Because if I take seriously what my father says—four, five—I'm off to hell, and if not and don't, then I'm bound for that other hell, the one up above.... The priests too should shut up and not talk so much... because *(she dries her eyes)*... if I don't marry Cocoliche, the priest will be to blame... the priest himself... who, when all is said and done, couldn't care less about us. Ay! Ay! Ay! Ay!

CRISTOBITA *(at the window with his Servant):* She's a juicy piece. You like her?

SERVANT *(trembling):* Yes, sir.

CRISTOBITA: The mouth's a bit big, but her body's as tasty as a cinnamon stick... though I still haven't closed the deal... I'd like to talk to her, but I don't want her getting too familiar. Familiarity breeds all the vices. And don't say you don't agree with me!

SERVANT (*trembling*): But, sir!

CRISTOBITA: There are just two ways to treat humans: either ignore them . . . or put them out of the way!

SERVANT: Oh, my God!

CRISTOBITA: Listen, you really like her!

SERVANT: Your Grace deserves still better.

CRISTOBITA: She's a tasty hunk of woman. And all my own! All mine! (*Exit*)

ROSITA: That's all I had to see! I am in despair. I'll go and poison myself right away by swallowing matches or some corrosive sublimate.

(*The wall clock opens and an* HOUR *appears, dressed in yellow and wearing a bustle.*)

HOUR (*using both a bell and her mouth*): Ding dong! One o'clock. Be patient, Rosita. What will you do? Little do you know of the turns things take. While the sun shines here, it's raining elsewhere. What do you know of tomorrow's winds that may rise and spin the weather vane around on your tile roof? Since I come around every day, I will remind you of this when you are old and have forgotten this moment. Let water run and starlight have its way. Have patience, Rosita. Ding dong! One o'clock (*clock closes*)

ROSITA: One o'clock. But damn it, if I ever get hungry again!

VOICE: The sighs of my love
        float through the air.

ROSITA: Now I see them come in . . . the sighs of my love.

(*The wall clock opens again and the* HOUR *appears, asleep. Only the bell makes a sound.*)

ROSITA (*tearfully*): The sighs of my love . . .

Curtain

SECOND SCENE

The little theatre represents an Andalusian village square. To the right the house of Mistress Rosita. There should be an enormous palm tree and a bench. Cocoliche appears on the left, serenading with a guitar in his hands and wrapped in a dark green cape with black piping. He is wearing a folk costume of the early nineteenth century and his flat little Calaña hat set at a jaunty angle.

COCOLICHE: No sign of Rosita. She's afraid of the moon. The moon is a terrible thing for secret lovers. *(He whistles)* The whistle resounds like a pebble of music against the window glass of her balcony. Yesterday she wore a black ribbon in her hair. She told me: a black ribbon in my hair is like a bruise on a fruit. Be sad if you see me: the black spot will soon spread down to my feet. Something bad is happening.

(The little balcony with its flower pots glows with a soft light.)

ROSITA *(within)*: With the vito, vito, vito,
　　　　　　　with the vito I expire.

COCOLICHE *(drawing near)*: Why not come out?

ROSITA *(in the balcony, very affectedly poetic)*: The Moorish wind is now spinning all the weather vanes in Andalusia. They'll go on spinning this way for a hundred years.

COCOLICHE: What are you trying to say?

ROSITA: To look to the left side and right side of here so your heart may learn to be serene.

COCOLICHE: I don't understand you.

ROSITA: What I am about to tell you bears a sharp sting. That's what I am preparing you for. *(pause and* ROSITA *comically bursts into a flood of tears)* I cannot marry you!

COCOLICHE: Rosita!!!

ROSITA: You are the apple of my eye, but I am not free to marry you. *(weeping)*

COCOLICHE: Would you enter the convent? Have I done something wrong?... Oh my oh my oh my! *(He weeps in a comical and childish way.)*

ROSITA: You'll find out later. Goodbye for now.

COCOLICHE *(screaming and stamping his foot on the ground)*: No, no, no, no!

ROSITA: Goodbye, my father is calling me. *(The balcony closes.)*

COCOLICHE *(alone)*: My ears are ringing as though I were on top of a mountain. It's like I was made of paper and about to be consumed by the little flame of my own heart. But this can't happen. No, no, no, and no! *(stamping on the ground)* And she doesn't want to marry me? When I bought her that locket from the Mairena Fair, she touched my cheek with her hand. When I gave her that rose-colored shawl, she looked at me that certain way...and when I brought her that mother-of-pearl fan with Pedro Romero opening his matador cape, she kissed me once for every rib of the fan. Yes, sir! So many kisses! It would have been better if I'd been split in half by a lightning bolt. Ay, ay, ay! *(He weeps in perfect rhythm.)*

(Enter on the left four young men, dressed in folk costumes. One of them has a guitar, another a tambourine. They sing.)

My true love always bathes
in the Guadalquivir.
My true love stitches her kerchief
in brilliant crimson silk.

YOUTH 1: It's Cocoliche.

YOUTH 2: Why are you crying? Up with you, and stop worrying if some bird in the woods hops from one tree to the next.

COCOLICHE: Leave me be!

YOUTH 3: No, we can't. Come along, and let the country air blow your cares away.

YOUTH 1: Let's go, come on. *(They take him away, with music and song.)*

(The stage is left empty. The moon lights up the broad village square.)

(DOÑA ROSITA's house door opens and her FATHER appears, dressed in gray, with a rose-colored wig and face to match. CRISTOBITA is dressed in green, and with a huge pot belly and noticeably hunchbacked. He wears a necklace, a bracelet with tiny bells and a billy club which he uses as a walking stick.)

CRISTOBITA: So we've closed the deal, right?

FATHER: Yes, sir, but...

CRISTOBITA: No ifs or buts about it—we closed the deal! I give you five hundred dollars to free you of your debts and you give me your daughter Rosita...and you should be happy because...she's a little overripe.

FATHER: She's sixteen years old.

CRISTOBITA: And I say that she's overripe, and that's what she is!

FATHER: Yes, that's . . . it, sir.

CRISTOBITA: But nevertheless she's a pretty piece. What the devil! A *boccato di cardinale.*

FATHER *(gravely):* Does your honor speak Italian?

CRISTOBITA: No. As a boy I was in Italy and in France, serving a certain Don Pantaloon. . . . But that has nothing at all to do with you!

FATHER: No . . . no, sir. . . . It's nothing to me.

CRISTOBITA: So by tomorrow afternoon I want the ceremony over with.

FATHER: That's impossible, Don Cristóbal.

CRISTOBITA: Who's that just said no to me? I don't know why I haven't chucked you into the gully where I've chucked so many before. This billy club you see here has killed thousands of Frenchmen, Hungarians, Italians. . . . I have the list of them at home. Obey me or you'll go waltzing off with the rest of them. It's been a while since this club of mine had a workout and it's dying to jump out of my hand. So watch out!

FATHER: Yes, sir . . .

CRISTOBITA: Now, take the money. That girl just cost me plenty. . . mighty plenty. But in the end, what's done is done. I'm a man never goes back on his word.

FATHER *(aside):* Good God, to whom am I handing over my daughter?

CRISTOBITA: What are you mumbling? . . . Let's go drum up the priest!

FATHER *(trembling):* Let us go.

ROSITA: With the vito, vito, vito,
      with the vito I shall expire.
      Every hour with my deario,
      I get closer to the fire!

CRISTOBITA: What was that?

FATHER: My dear daughter singing. . . . It's a lovely song!

CRISTOBITA: Bah! I'll teach her one that'll give her voice a workout, more natural, a song that goes like this:
               The frog sings brackety acks,
               brackety, brackety acks . . .

(curtain)

THIRD SCENE

A village tavern. In the back, barrels and blue vats against the white walls. An old bullfight poster and three oil lamps. Night. The tavern keeper is behind the bar. He is a man in shirt sleeves, cowlick hair, flat nose. His name is Espantanublos. On the right, a classic gang of smugglers, wearing velvet, with beards and blunderbusses, throwing dice and singing.

SMUGGLER 1: What a fine little road
      to Gibraltar from Cádiz.

      The sea knows I go
      by my sighs.

      Ay maid, my maid,
      and all the boats in Malaga harbor!

      To Seville from Cádiz,
      the stretches of lime trees!

      The lime trees know me
      by my sighs.

      Ah maid, my maid,
      all the boats in Malaga harbor!

SMUGGLER 2: Here there, Espantanublos! This gay little ditty opened my thirsty throat. Bring on the Malaga wine!

ESPANTANUBLOS (*lazily*): Right away!

(*Through the center door appears a YOUNG MAN wrapped in a wide blue capo. He wears a straight flat hat. Suspense. He comes in and sits down at a table on the left, without revealing his face.*)

ESPANTANUBLOS: Does your grace want something to drink?

YOUNG MAN: Oh, no!

ESPANTANUBLOS: Have you been here a while?

YOUNG MAN: Oh, no!

ESPANTANUBLOS: He seems to be sighing.

YOUNG MAN: Ah, me! Ah, me!

SMUGGLER 1: Who is he?

ESPANTANUBLOS: I haven't a clue.

SMUGGLER 2: What if he's a . . .

SMUGGLER 1: We'd better be going.

SMUGGLER 2: It's a very clear night.

SMUGGLER 1: With stars all over the houses.

SMUGGLER 2: By morning we'll be within sight of the sea.

> (*They leave and the* YOUNG MAN *is alone. His little face is hardly visible. The stage is lit up by a sharp blue light.*)

YOUNG MAN: I find the town is whiter, much whiter. When I looked at it from the mountain, the light got in through my eyes and went straight down to my feet. We Andalusians white-wash everything, even ourselves, right down to the bone. But something is trembling inside me. Good God, but I shouldn't have come!

ESPANTANUBLOS: He's worse off than Don Tancredo, but I . . . (*In the street, loud voices and guitars are heard. He is going out.*) What's up? (COCOLICHE *enters at the head of a gang of boys.*)

COCOLICHE (*drunk*): Espantanublos, give us some wine till it comes out of our eyes. It will color our tears—tears of topaz and ruby. . . . Ay, my friends, my friends!

YOUTH 1: So young and so sad! One thing we won't tolerate is for you to be sad.

ALL: Say that again!

COCOLICHE: She used to tell me such precious things! She would say: Your lips are red as two strawberries still ripening, and . . .

YOUTH 1 (*interrupting him*): Certainly a romantic woman. That's just the reason I wouldn't feel sad. Don Cristobita is a fat drunken old sluggard, who won't take long to . . .

ALL: Bravo!

YOUTH 2: Who won't take long to . . . (*laughter*)

ESPANTANUBLOS: Now, gentlemen . . .

YOUTH 2: And now for a toast.

YOUTH 1: I toast what I toast because I must be toasting. Cocoliche: at midnight his door will come open and the rest will follow.

ALL: ¡Olé! (*A burst of guitar music*)

YOUTH 2: And I toast Doña Rosita.

YOUTH 1 (*standing*): To Doña Rosita!

YOUTH 2: And may her future husband explode like an overstuffed puppet! (*laughter*).

YOUNG MAN (*approaching, still muffled*): Just a moment! I'm a stranger and would like to know who is this Rosita you toast so gaily.

COCOLICHE: A stranger, and this interests you so much?

YOUNG MAN: It just might.

COCOLICHE: Close the door, Espantanublos. This gentleman seems to be cold, although we've almost reached the month of May.

YOUTH 2: Especially around the gills.

YOUNG MAN: I come here to ask you a decent question and you answer me with a lot of hoopla. It seems to me your jokes are getting out of hand.

COCOLICHE: Then what is it to you who this woman is?

YOUNG MAN: More than you'd believe.

COCOLICHE: All right, then: the woman is Doña Rosita, from the heart of town, the best singer in Andalusia, my ... and yes, my fiancée.

YOUTH 2 (*coming forward*): And since she's about to marry Don Cristobita, this young man, well ... you can imagine the rest yourself.

ALL: ¡Olé! ¡Olé! (*laughter*)

YOUNG MAN (*sorrowfully*): Excuse me. Your conversation interested me because I once had a sweetheart who was also called Rosita ...

YOUTH 2: Who's not your sweetheart any more?

YOUNG MAN: No. Women nowadays seem to go for young whippersnappers. Good night. (*starts to leave*)

YOUTH 2: Sir, before you go, I'd like to have you join us in a glass of wine. (*He holds it out*)

YOUNG MAN (*at the door, nervously*): Many thanks, but I don't drink. Good night, gentlemen. (*aside as he leaves*) I don't know how I could contain myself.

ESPANTANUBLOS: Now who the devil is that guy and what's he come here for?

YOUTH 2: That's just what I want to ask you. Who is this stranger, all muffled up in some disguise?

YOUTH 1: You're a poor barkeeper—not knowing that!

COCOLICHE: That man! I'm worried, worried . . .

(All are uneasy, speaking in hushed voices.)

YOUTH 2 *(from the doorway):* Gentlemen: it's Don Cristobita coming to the tavern.

COCOLICHE: Good chance to break his head.

ESPANTANUBLOS: I don't want any brawls in my place. And so you can all be on your way, right now.

YOUTH 1: Forget your quarrels, Cocoliche. Forget them now.

(Two youths carry COCOLICHE *away and the other two hide behind the wine casks. The stage remains silent.)*

CRISTOBITA *(in the doorway):* Brrrrrruuuuu!

ESPANTANUBLOS *(terrified):* Good evening.

CRISTOBITA: You have a lot of wine here, right?

ESPANTANUBLOS: Any kind you desire, señor.

CRISTOBITA: Well, I want it all, all of it!

YOUTH 1 *(from a corner):* Cristobita! *(falsetto)*

CRISTOBITA: What? Who said that?

ESPANTANUBLOS: Some little dog out there in the orchard.

CRISTOBITA *(grabbing his club and singing):*
If you're a fox, hide your tail.
This is the club to make you wail.

ESPANTANUBLOS *(uneasy):* I have sweet wine . . . white wine . . . sour wine . . . a wine of a wine . . .

CRISTOBITA: And dirt cheap, right? You're all a bunch of crooks! Say it.

ESPANTANUBLOS *(trembling):* A bunch of crooks.

CRISTOBITA: Tomorrow I marry Missy Rosita, and I want there to be lots of wine to . . . to drink it all up myself.

YOUTH 1 *(from the wine cask):* Cristobita to guzzle it all and fall asleep.

YOUTH 2 *(from another cask):* Guzzle it up and fall asleep.

CRISTOBITA: Brrrr. Br, br, br. Do these wine barrels talk or are you pulling my leg?

ESPANTANUBLOS: Me? me? . . .

CRISTOBITA: Smell the club! What's the smell?

ESPANTANUBLOS: It smells of . . . well . . .

CRISTOBITA: Tell me!

ESPANTANUBLOS: Of brains!

CRISTOBITA: And what did you think? *(furiously)* As for guzzling and sleeping, let's see now who guzzles and sleeps, you or me!

ESPANTANUBLOS: But Don Cristóbal, but Don Cristóbal . . .

YOUTH 2 *(from the cask):* Cristo-balloon
　　　　　　　　　　　pot-bellied buffoon

CRISTOBITA *(swinging his club):* Scoundrel, your time has come, you damn rogue you . . .

ESPANTANUBLOS: Oh Don Cristóbal, apple of my eye!

YOUTH 2: Pot-bellied buffoon.

CRISTOBITA: You dare come at me? We'll see now. Take that, you pot-belly, pot-belly, pot!

(Both of them exit, CRISTOBITA flailing with his club, ESPANTANUBLOS screaming like a rat. The YOUTHS crack up with laughter from their wine casks. Music.)

Curtain

FOURTH SCENE

The village square, as before, but far less illuminated by moonlight. The yellow palm stands out against a starless blue sky. The drunken youths enter on the left, dragging tipsy COCOLICHE along with them.

YOUTH 1: Don Cristobita, that so and so, has an awful temper.

YOUTH 2: And the beating he gave that poor tavern keeper!

YOUTH 1: Tell me, what do we do with this fellow?

YOUTH 2: Let's just drop him here, and don't worry. He'll wake when the night dew hits his face. *(They leave)*

(Flute music that quickly approaches, bringing MOSQUITO onstage. The light brightens. Seeing him asleep, he draws closer to COCOLICHE and blows the toy trumpet in his ear. COCOLICHE swats at it. MOSQUITO steps back.)

MOSQUITO: He doesn't know what's happening—naturally, he's just a child. But it's a sure thing that Mistress Rosita's heart—a tiny heart, hardly this big—is slipping away from him. *(laughs)* Doña Rosita's soul is like those little mother-of-pearl boats from Valencia sold at the fairs, with a tiny scissors and a thimble inside. Now he'll mark the stiff sail "Souvenir" and it will sail farther and farther away. *(He leaves, playing his little horn and the stage grows darker once more.)*

(Enter the YOUNG MAN *with the muffled face and a youth from the village.)*

YOUNG MAN: Now I'm glad I came but I'm still so angry I can hardly speak. You say she's getting married?

YOUTH: Tomorrow, with a certain Don Cristóbal, rich, lazy, and so brutal that even his shadow tears things to bits. But I think she has forgotten you.

YOUNG MAN: That's not possible. She loved me and that was just . . .

YOUTH: Five years back.

YOUNG MAN: You're right.

YOUTH: Why did you leave her?

YOUNG MAN: I don't know. Things here got me down so much. Going to and from the harbor, you know! I had the idea that in the world bells were always ringing and that along the roads were white hotels and blonde girls with their sleeves rolled up to their elbows. But there's nothing like that. It's all very boring!

YOUTH: And what are you thinking of doing?

YOUNG MAN: I want to see her.

YOUTH: That's impossible. You don't know Don Cristóbal.

YOUNG MAN: But I must see her, at whatever cost.

(Enter CANSA-ALMAS, *stage right.)*

YOUTH: Ah, that's someone who can be of use; it's Cansa-Almas, the shoemaker. *(calls out)* Cansa-Almas!

CANSA-ALMAS: What . . . what . . . what?

YOUTH: Look here. You're going to be useful to this gentleman.

CANSA-ALMAS: To whom? . . . To . . . whom?

YOUNG MAN *(showing his face):* Look at me!

CANSA-ALMAS: Currito!

CURRITO: Yes, Currito from the Harbor.

CANSA-ALMAS *(poking him in the belly):* Why, you little scrapper, you got fat!

YOUTH: Isn't it true you're going to try on Rosita the bride's shoes tomorrow?

CANSA-ALMAS: Yes... yes... yes...

YOUTH: Well, you must let this fellow take your place.

CANSA-ALMAS: No, no—I don't want any trouble.

CURRITO: You'll see I'll pay you well. Come, for your childrens' sake, I beg you to let me do it.

YOUTH: Besides, he will pay you well. He has money.

CANSA-ALMAS: That's enough. What'll I do? I'll let you! I'll stay home... And it's true... *(taking out a big bandana)* your father really loved me, a lot, a whole lot.

CURRITO *(embracing him):* Thank you, many thanks!

CANSA-ALMAS: Are you going back to selling oranges? Oh, how wonderfully you would shout out your wares. Oranges... oraangesss. ... *(They leave.)*

(The moonlight starts to flood the stage and guitar music is strummed in the air.)

COCOLICHE *(dreaming):* Cristobita will beat you, my love. Cristobita has a green paunch and a green hump. His snoring at night won't let you sleep. And I should be covering you with many kisses! What misery it was seeing you with a bow in your hair. The blackness that will spread down to your feet!

(The melody of the vito invades the stage. An apparition appears on stage right, out of COCOLICHE's dreams. It's DOÑA ROSITA, dressed in dark blue, with a crown of spikenard on her head and a silver knife in her hand.)

SPECTER OF DOÑA ROSITA *(singing):* With the vito, vito, vito,
                with the vito, vito, clearly
                every hour I am sailing
                farther, farther from you.

(The yellow palm is full of little silver lights, and everything takes on an intensely theatrical bluish tinge.)

COCOLICHE: Holy Virgin! *(He stands up, but at the same moment everything disappears.)* I'm awake. There's no question but that I'm awake. There she was, in mourning clothes. I still seem to have her in view . . . and that music . . .

(Now from the balcony comes the actual voice of ROSITA, *singing because she can't sleep.)*

ROSITA: With the vito, vito, vito,
  with the vito, I shall expire . . .
  Every hour with my dearie,
  I get closer to the fire!

COCOLICHE: This is the first time I ever really cried. I tell you truly: the first time!

Curtain

FIFTH SCENE

The scene is an Andalusian street with white-washed houses. In the first house, a shoemaker's shop; in the second, a barber shop, with mirror and chair in the open. Farther down, a huge doorway with this sign: "Inn of All the Disenchanted of the World!" On the door a huge heart pierced by seven swords. It is morning. In his shoemaker's shop CANSA-ALMAS *is seated at his workbench sewing a riding boot, while waiting nearby in his small shop is* FÍGARO, *dressed in green, wearing a black hairnet and side-locks, sharpening a straight razor on a long strop.*

FÍGARO: I'm expecting a great visit today.

CANSA-ALMAS: What vis- ? What vis- ?

(A flute backstage completes the sentence.)

FÍGARO: Don Cristobita is coming. Don Cristobita, the billy-club man!

CANSA-ALMAS: Don't you th-? Don't you th-? *(The flute completes the sentence.)*

FÍGARO *(laughing):* Yes, yes, of course!

AN URCHIN: Shoemaker, aker, aker,
  put the awl
  through the hole.

FÍGARO: Oh, you little scoundrel, scoundrel! *(Exit, running after him.*

CURRITO THE HARBORMAN *enters on the other side. As always, he comes with his cape collar turned up; reaching stage center, he bumps into* FÍGARO, *who quickly turns around and comes back from the other side.)*

CURRITO: Slice me with that razor and I'll gouge out your eyes.

FÍGARO: Excuse me, m'sieu, do you need a shave? My barber shop...

(As the flute plays, FÍGARO *exhibits his own talents in dumbshow.)*

CURRITO: Go and get yourself cudgeled!

FÍGARO *(imitating* CURRITO's *street-call):* Oraaanges, oraaanges! *(He whistles.)*

CURRITO *(He arrives at the shoemaker's.):* Cansa-Almas, give me the little shoes and the shoebox.

CANSA-ALMAS *(trembling):* But...but...but...

CURRITO: Hand them over, I tell you!

CANSA-ALMAS: Take them.... Take them...

FÍGARO *(capering):* Loosening and tightening,
I lost my little thimble;
loosening and tightening,
I found it—that was simple!

CURRITO *(caressing the little rose-colored shoes):*
Oh, the dear little shoes
of my mistress Rosita!
Wouldn't anyone die to see them
on the legs of such a creature?

CANSA-ALMAS: Oh leave me alone. Just leave me alone.

(He continues to work with his awl.)

CURRITO *(enraptured with her shoes):* They're like two wine cups, a nun's double pin cushions, and like two little sighs.

FÍGARO: Something's happening. Undoubtedly something is going on! The town smells of news. Ah, the new thing! But it will now come to my barbershop.

CURRITO *(leaving, shoes in hand):* Is it possible that you are not mine, Rosita? *(kisses the slippers)* They are like the moon's two tears at eventide, like two little towers in the land of the elves. *(a loud kiss)* Like two... *(exit)*

FÍGARO: Now I'll find out all that's happening. News reaches the world after it has been classified at the barber shop. Barbershops are the clearing house of the news. This razor that you see slashes through the shell of any secret.... We barbers have a keen scent for dark words and mysterious looks. Naturally we're the head mayors, and because we're making inroads through forests of hair we get to know what is being thought within. What pretty little stories I could tell about the ugly old snoozers in barbers' chairs!

CRISTOBITA (*entering*): I want a shave right away—yes, sure, right now, because I am going to be married! Brrrr! And I am not inviting anyone. You are, all of you, thieves!

(CANSA-ALMAS *shuts the door and sticks his head through the little window.*)

FÍGARO: They are.

CRISTOBITA (*raising his club*): You are!

FÍGARO (*very positively*): They are (*pointing to his watch*)—clock hands—pointing to ten!

CRISTOBITA: Ten o'clock or eleven—I want a shave this minute.

CANSA-ALMAS: What a bad joker he is!

CRISTOBITA (*beating* CANSA-ALMAS *over the head*): Tit for tat! Take this, take that!

(CANSA-ALMAS, *pulling his head in, squeals like a rat.*)

CRISTOBITA: Let's go now. (*sits down*)

FÍGARO: What a wonderful head of hair you have! But how magnificent! A living model.

CRISTOBITA: Start shaving!

FÍGARO (*working*): Tra-la-la-la-la.

CRISTOBITA: You nick me and I'll slice you from top to toe—from top to toe, I said, and from top to toe it'll be.

FÍGARO: Excellent, admirable. I am enchanted. Tra-la-la-la-la.

(*The door of the inn opens and a young woman appears, dressed in yellow, with a bright red rose in her hair. Inside the inn door an* OLD BEGGAR *takes his place with an accordion.*)

YOUNG WOMAN (*singing and playing castanets*): I have my eyes nailed
                                        on that young man
                                        slim-waisted,
                                        dark and tall.

On his flower,
brilliant flower,
by the olive tree green
where the maid sits combing
sunlight in her hair.

ALL: On the flower,
brilliant flower,
by the olive tree green
where the maid sits combing
sunlight in her hair.

YOUNG WOMAN: In the olive grove there
I await you, dear,
with a jug of wine red
and black coarse bread.
On the flower,
brilliant flower,
by the olive tree green
where the maid sits combing
sunlight in her hair.

ALL: On the flower,
brilliant flower,
by the olive tree green
where the maid sits combing
sunlight in her hair.

FÍGARO (*looks at the* YOUNG WOMAN): To the flower, and what a flower!
Ha! Ha! Ha! Cansa-Almas, come over here quickly!

(*The* YOUNG WOMAN *stands there looking astonished at* CRISTOBITA *asleep.*)

CRISTOBITA (*snoring*): Brrrr, brrrr

CANSA-ALMAS (*fearful*): No, I don't want to come. (*His head is stuck out the window.*)

FÍGARO: That's so wonderful! Just as I imagined it would be. But how really stupendous. Cristobita's head is made of wood. It's poplar wood. Ha, ha, ha! (*The* YOUNG WOMAN *comes closer.*) Just look at it—look at all the coats of paint on it! Ha, ha, ha!

CANSA-ALMAS (*set to leave*): He's going to wake up.

FÍGARO: He's got two knots in his forehead, and that's where he sweats . . . the rosin! That was the news! The great new thing!

CRISTOBITA *(beginning to stir):* Hurry up now, brrr, brrr, hurry.

FÍGARO: Yes, excellency, yes!

YOUNG WOMAN: O I have my eyes nailed
    on that young man
    slim-waisted
    dark and tall.
    On his flower,
    brilliant flower,
    by the olive tree green
    where the maid sits combing
    sunlight in her hair.

ALL: *(Gathered around* CRISTOBITA *asleep, and very softly so he won't hear it, but still full of fun.)*

On his flower, etc.

(Through the Inn window, a MAJA WITH BEAUTY MARKS *looks out, opening and closing her fan.)*

Curtain

SIXTH SCENE

House of DOÑA ROSITA. *In the front balconies two large wardrobes with shutters in the upper section. A metal oil lamp hangs from the ceiling. The walls a very light shade of rose-colored sugar. A portrait of Santa Rosa de Lima hangs on the front door, under an arch of lemons.* DOÑA ROSITA *appears, dressed in rose. A great bridal gown full of ruffles and elaborate ribbons and sashes. Above a low-cut neckline, a choker of black jet.*

ROSITA: Everything's over—lost and gone! I'm going to my execution as if I were Marianita Pineda. She had on a little iron choker for her wedding with death, and I will have on me a necklace..., a necklace from Cristobita. *(cries and sings)*
    A speckled bird once sat
    in a green lemon tree,

    (a catch in her throat)

    its beak stirring a leaf,
    its tail, the blossom.
      Ay! Ay!
    When will I see my love?

(A Voice is heard singing offstage.)

VOICE: Rosita, only to see you—
    the tips of your toes,
    if only they'd let me,
    we'd see what's to see.

ROSITA: Oh, my dear Santa Rosa—whose voice is that?

CURRITO *(muffled, appears at the door):* Can one come in?

ROSITA *(astonished):* Who are you?

CURRITO: One man among many men.

ROSITA: But . . . do you have a face?

CURRITO: Well-known to those little eyes of yours.

ROSITA: That voice . . .

CURRITO *(opening his cape):* Look at me!

ROSITA *(frightened):* Currito!

CURRITO: Yes, Currito—who went out into the world and returns now to marry you.

ROSITA: No, no! Good God, go away! I'm promised to somebody else, and besides, I don't love you. You've left me before. Now I love Cristobita. Go away, go away!

CURRITO: I am not going away. Why did I come here?

ROSITA: Oh, how unfortunate I am. I have a little watch and a little silver mirror, but plagued with disaster now!

CURRITO: Come away with me. Looking at you I grow crazy with jealousy.

ROSITA: You want to ruin me, villain!

CURRITO *(coming closer, to embrace her):* Rosita, my own!

ROSITA: People are coming. Go away, you bandit! Delinquent!

FATHER *(entering):* What's happening?

CURRITO: I come to Mistress Rosita to try on her wedding shoes because Cansa-Almas couldn't be here. They're beautiful shoes, like for a royal princess.

FATHER: Try them on!

(DOÑA ROSITA sits down. CURRITO kneels at her feet and her father reads a newspaper.)

CURRITO: Ah, such a lovely lily-white leg!

ROSITA *(under her breath):* You dog!

CURRITO *(aloud):* Raise your skirt a little.

ROSITA: There you are.

>   *(CURRITO puts on the shoe.)*

CURRITO: Let me see—a bit more?

ROSITA: That's enough, little shoemaker.

CURRITO: Another little bit?

FATHER *(from his chair):* Do what he asks, girl—a bit higher.

ROSITA: Ay!

CURRITO: Still a bit more! *(He keeps studying ROSITA's leg.)* Still more, again!

FATHER: I'm going. The shoes are quite pretty. On my way I'll shut the door. It's still a little chilly here. *(He goes to the main door.)* It's hard shutting it. It must be it was mouldy.

CURRITO: O what a pretty foot
    has your Grace!
    O how prettily
    it fits your grace!

ROSITA: Evil man! Jew dog!

CURRITO: Rosita, my Maytime rose!

ROSITA *(screeching softly):* Oh me, oh my, oh my! *(running around the stage)* Don Cristóbal's coming. Run out through here! *(They find the door is shut tight.)* But how did my father come to lock it?

CURRITO *(trembling):* The fact is . . .

ROSITA: I feel his footsteps on the staircase. Guide me, Santa Rosa! *(CURRITO meanwhile tries to open the door.)* Ah! Come this way. *(She opens the wardrobe on the right side and hides him inside.)* That's it now. I thought I was done for.

CRISTOBITA *(offstage):* Brrrrr!

ROSITA *(singing on the verge of tears):* While the speckled bird's
            alighted on the lemon tree,
            ah, when will I my true love see!

(choking)

CRISTOBITA *(at the door):* I smell human flesh
right at my feet.
Give 'em up to me
or it's you I'll eat.

ROSITA: What things you say, Cristobita!

CRISTOBITA: I don't want you talking to anyone! Nobody at all. Now
I've told you! Ah, how tasty you are! What great little buns you
have!

ROSITA: Cristobita, I . . .

CRISTOBITA: Let's get married right away. . . . Listen, you've never seen
me kill anyone with my club. No? Well, now you will. I go bing,
bang, buff! . . . and over into the gully.

ROSITA: Yes, it's very pretty.

ACOLYTE *(through the window):* The priest his reverence says: you
should come when you are ready.

CRISTOBITA: Well, let's go. Olé! Olé! Let's go! *(He grabs a bottle and
drinks while he dances.)*

ROSITA: Well then. I'll put on my veil.

CRISTOBITA: I too will put on: I'm going to put on my great hat and tie
the ribbons on my club. . . . Now I'm coming. *(He leaves, dancing.)*

CURRITO *(looking out of the shutter of the wardrobe):* Open up for me.

*(*ROSITA *goes toward the wardrobe when* COCOLICHE *enters in a great
leap through the window.)*

ROSITA: Ay! *(She turns to him and falls into his arms.)* There's no one in
the world I love other than you. *(*COCOLICHE *embraces her.)*

COCOLICHE: Darling!

CURRITO *(in the wardrobe):* Oh, I thought so. You are a lost woman!

COCOLICHE: What does this mean?

ROSITA: I am going to go crazy!

COCOLICHE: What are you doing in that rat hole of yours? Come into
the light of day like a man. *(beating against the wardrobe)*

ROSITA: Have mercy on me!

COCOLICHE: Mercy on you? Oh, you miserable slut!

CURRITO: I would like to strangle you both.

COCOLICHE: Get out of there at once! Break down the door! Coward!

ROSITA: Cristobita's coming! Mercy me, Cristobita's coming!

CRISTOBITA: Ooooopen!

COCOLICHE: Let him come, and see how his bride-be-be is carrying on with her lover.

ROSITA: I'll explain everything to you, my love. Run!

CRISTOBITA *(offstage)*: Rosita...! Chiquita...!

ROSITA: There's no time. Here! *(She opens the other wardrobe and hides* COCOLICHE, *then puts on her rose-colored veil.)* I'm dying. *(She pretends she's singing.)*

CRISTOBITA *(entering)*: What was all that noise?

ROSITA: They... were wedding guests waiting at the door.

CRISTOBITA: I don't want guests!

ROSITA: But look... they're here!

CRISTOBITA: Well, if they're here, let them take off. Let them go away! *(aside)* And I'll find out what the noise is about. *(aloud)* Let's go, Rosita. Huh? Oh, how appetizing she looks!

(The main door opens and the wedding guests appear; they are carrying huge hoops of paper roses of all sorts, through which DON CRISTÓBAL *and* ROSITA *pass.)*

GUESTS: Long live the newlyweds.

ALL: Long life to you. *(music)*

(The heads of CURRITO *and* COCOLICHE *appear through the shutters.)*

CURRITO: I am going to burst!

COCOLICHE: So you're that woman's lover! I'll have it out with you later, face to face.

CURRITO: Wherever you like, you scoundrel!

COCOLICHE: If this wardrobe wasn't made of iron...

CURRITO: Ha, ha!

COCOLICHE: I'd gladly snap off your nose in one bite! *("Long live the newlyweds. Long life to them!" is heard from offstage.)* Now they're about to be married. She's forgotten me forever now. *(weeps)*

CURRITO *(declaiming)*: I came to this village to learn how easy it is to forget!

COCOLICHE: She'll never again call me "Little Fruitface," nor I call her "Little Almond-head"!

CURRITO: I'll go away forever, forever!

COCOLICHE: Ay, ay, ay!

CURRITO: Ingrate, ingrate, ingrate!

(Church bells, fireworks and music heard from out of doors.)

COCOLICHE: I can't go on living any longer!

CURRITO: I'll never look at another woman again!

(The two puppets weep.)

MOSQUITO *(entering on the left):* My friends, there's no need to cry. The earth has white roads, smooth roads, foolish roads. But now, my boys, why all this squandering of pearls! You are not princes. After all is said and done, the moon doesn't always wane, nor does the breeze always fall, nor the breeze rise. *(He plays his toy trumpet and leaves.)* Neither come nor go, come nor go . . .

(COCOLICHE and CURRITO heave a loud sigh and stare at one another.)

(The main door suddenly opens and the wedding cortege appears. DON CRISTÓBAL and MISTRESS ROSITA take leave of them at the door and close it. Music and church bells in the distance.)

CRISTOBITA: Ay, Rosita of my heart! Ay, Rosita!

ROSITA: Now he'll kill me with his club.

CRISTOBITA: Are you sick? It seems you're sighing! But that's because you like me. I am old and understand such things. Look at this suit I've got! And these boots! Tra-lee, tra-la! Bring on the sweets and the wine! . . . Lots of wine! *(A SERVANT enters with some bottles. CRISTOBITA takes one and begins to drink.)* Ah, pretty Rosita! Chiquita, my little almond! I am very handsome, right? I'll give you a kiss! Here, here . . . *(He kisses her. At that moment COCOLICHE and CURRITO look out of their shutters and cry out in rage.)* What's that? Is there something fearful about this house? *(He grabs his club.)*

ROSITA: No, no, Cristóbal! It's the termites, it's the children in the street . . .

CRISTOBITA: It's a fearful lot of noise they're making, caramba! Lots of noise they're making!

ROSITA *(terrified but pretending):* When are you going to tell me the stories you promised?

CRISTOBITA: Ha, ha, ha! They're very pretty, just as pretty as that poppy blossom face of yours. *(Drinks)* It's the story of Don Tancred, mounted on his pedastal. You know? Hoo-hoo! And the story of Don Juan Tenorio, cousin of Don Tancredo and my cousin. Yes, sir. My cousin! Say it: My cousin!

ROSITA: Your cousin!

CRISTOBITA: Rosa, Rosa, tell me something!

ROSITA: I love you, Cristobita.

CRISTOBITA: Olé! Olé! *(He kisses her. Another scream comes out of the wardrobes.)* That's the end of it, the end, the dead end! Brrrr!

ROSITA: Ay! Don't take on so!

CRISTOBITA *(with his club):* Whoever's inside there, out with you!

ROSITA: Look, don't take on so. A bird just flew by this moment past the window with such wings . . . big as this!

CRISTOBITA *(imitating her):* Big as this, big as this! You think I'm blind?

ROSITA: You don't love me! *(She cries.)*

CRISTOBITA *(softened):* Should I believe you . . . or not believe you? *(He drops the club.)*

ROSITA *(putting on):* It's such a perfectly clear night over the rooftops. It's the hour when the children are counting the stars and the old people fall asleep in their saddles.

(CRISTOBITA sits down, puts his feet up on the table, and starts to drink.)

CRISTOBITA: I'd like to be made totally of wine and drink myself up. Hooo! And my belly become a pie, a great big red pie, with sweet potatoes and plums. *(The puppets looking out of their shutters are sighing.)* Who's sighing?

ROSITA: I am. . . . It's me remembering back to my childhood.

CRISTOBITA: When I was a child, they gave me a pie bigger than the moon and I ate it up all by myself. . . . Hooo! ! All alone.

ROSITA *(romantically):* In the mountains of Córdoba, there are shadows in the olive orchards, flattened-out shadows, dead shadows that never go away. Oh, who wouldn't be under those roots! In the mountains of Granada there are feet of light, hair-dos of snow. Oh, who wouldn't lie under those springs. Seville has no mountains.

CRISTOBITA: No, it has no mountains, no . . .

ROSITA: Long orange-colored roads. Oh, who wouldn't get lost upon them!

(CRISTOBITA, *listening to her like one who listens to a violinist, has fallen asleep, a bottle in his hand.*)

CURRITO *(very softly):* Open up!

COCOLICHE: Don't open mine! I want to die in here.

ROSITA: Quiet, for God's sake!

(MOSQUITO *enters and begins to play his toy trumpet around* CRISTOBITA, *who tries to brush him away.*)

CURRITO: I'm going off to where nobody will ever see me.

ROSITA: I never loved you. You are a wanderer.

COCOLICHE: What's this I hear?

ROSITA: Only you, my love!

COCOLICHE: But you're already married!

CRISTOBITA: Brrr. Pesky mosquitos! Pesky mosquitos!

ROSITA: Santa Rosa, don't let him wake up! *(She turns to a wardrobe and carefully opens it.)*

(*This whole scene is played very rapidly and sotto voce.*)

CURRITO *(leaving his wardrobe):* Farewell forever, ingrate! My punishment is I'll never forget you! *(At this moment* MOSQUITO *aims a loud trumpet blast at* CRISTOBITA's *head and wakens him.*)

CRISTOBITA: Ah, what, what! Impossible! Brrr!

CURRITO *(drawing out his dagger):* Be calm, dear sir, be calm!

CRISTOBITA: I shall kill you. I shall tear you to bits! I shall grind up your bones. And now you will pay for this, Mistress Rosita, fallen woman! Five hundred dollars you cost me. Brrr. Bing, bang, buff! I am choking with rage! What were you doing here?

CURRITO *(trembles):* What . . . whatever I please . . .

CRISTOBITA: Ahhrrr! So, it's whatever you please. Well, man! Take this, please! Please, take this whatever, and this, please! (CURRITO *strikes* CRISTÓBAL *with his dagger, but it gets stuck in the sluggard's chest in a peculiar way. During this scene,* ROSITA *has been opening the back door and at this time has succeeded in doing it, and* CURRITO, *pursued by* CRISTOBITA, *keeps telling him,* Take pleasure! Take pleasure!)

(ROSITA *lets out some piercing shrieks or laughs hysterically. All this time the characters should be helped along with flutes and whistles from a little orchestra.*)

COCOLICHE: Open this up for me because I'll kill him when he comes.

ROSITA: Let you out? (*She goes to open the door.*) No, I won't open it. He's coming now and will kill us all.

COCOLICHE: So we'll all die together!

ROSITA: Let you out? Ah, yes, I'll let you out. (*She opens it up.*) My darling sweetheart. Like the little tree in my garden.

COCOLICHE (*embracing her*): My carefully nurtured carnation! My little handful of cinnamon! (*Begins in the style of an idyllic operatic duet.*)

ROSITA: Go back home, for here I must die.

COCOCLICHE: I cannot possibly, Rosita among the flowers. On that star I shall build for you a swing and a balcony made all of silver, from which we'll view the trembling world dressed in moonlight.

ROSITA (*in her total joy, forgetting everything*): How romantic you are, my exquisite one! I am becoming a flower whose petals now are falling into your hands.

COCOLICHE: Day by day you become for me rosier and rosier; day by day you strip away veil after veil and surge up before me naked.

ROSITA (*placing her head on her sweetheart's chest*): A flight of one thousand birds has risen from your breast; when I look at you, my love, I seem to view it all from beneath a little fountain. (*Outside the voice of* CRISTOBITA, *and* ROSITA *is jolted out of her ecstacy.*) Fly away!

CRISTOBITA (*standing in the doorway stupefied*): Ahrrrrr! You have lovers by the pair! Get ready for the gully. Bing, bang, buff! (COCOLICHE *and* ROSITA *kiss desperately before* CRISTÓBAL.) Impossible! I who have slaughtered three hundred Englishmen, three hundred Constantinopolitans! You will remember me, yet! Ay! Ay! (*The club falls from his hand and a great popping of springs is heard.*) Ay, my pot belly, my belly! It's your fault I've been smashed and killed! Ay, I am dying! Ay, call the priest! Ay!

ROSITA (*screaming sharply and running across the stage, dragging her long train behind her*) Papaaaaaaaa! Paaaaaaa!

CRISTOBITA: Ahrrrrr! Bang! I'm done! (*He remains with his paunch up and his arms stretched high as he falls backward over the footlights.*)

ROSITA: He's dead! O, God in Heaven, what a compromising situation!

COCOLICHE *(approaching fearfully):* Listen, there's no blood in here!

ROSITA: He's got no blood?

COCOLICHE: Look! Look what's coming out of his belly button!

ROSITA: I'm afraid to.

COCOLICHE: Know something?

ROSITA: What?

COCOLICHE *(emphatically):* Cristóbal was not a person!

ROSITA: What? . . . Don't tell me any more! What an awful disappointment! Was he not really a person!

FATHER *(entering):* What's going on? What's going on?

(Enter various Puppets)

COCOLICHE: Look!

FATHER: He burst!

(The main door opens and the Puppets appear with torches; they wear red capes and black hats. MOSQUITO *is at the head carrying a banner and playing the toy trumpet. They carry an enormous coffin, in which are painted peppers and radishes instead of stars. The* PRIESTS *come in singing. Funeral march with flutes.)*

A PRIEST: Uri memento.
　　　　A man is dead.

ALL: He's done for, all done.
　　　Cristobalón.

A PRIEST: Whether we sing or not,
　　　　there's five bucks in the pot.

(On picking up CRISTOBITA, *a comical sound emerges from him, like a bassoon. Everyone steps back and* DOÑA ROSITA *weeps. They return and the sound is abated until her sighs are flute-like, and they throw him in the coffin. The* CORTEGE *circles the stage among the lamenting notes of the music.)*

COCOLICHE: I feel my chest is full of jingle bells, full of tiny little beating hearts. I'm a field of flowers!

ROSITA: My tears and kisses shall be yours, my carnation.

MOSQUITO *(leading the group):* This bread sack
　　　　　　　　we are burying

was the drunkard
Cristobita
and he will never
with his Brrrr
and raturrr
come back ever
ever raturrn
raturrn raturrn
raturrn again!

(COCOLICHE *and* ROSITA *are left embracing. Symphony.*)

Curtain

Play without a Title

CAST

Director	Voice (s)
Spectator (F) 1, 2	Spectator (M) 1, 2
Youth	Servant
Prompter	Actress
Nick Bottom	Man in Black
Woodsman	Stagehand
Woman 1, 2	Worker
Sylphs	Fairies

A gray curtain

DIRECTOR: Ladies and Gentlemen. I'm not about to raise the curtain to entertain an audience with some word-game or panorama of a house where nothing happens and where the spotlights are fixed just to amuse you and make you believe that that's what life is all about. No. The poet with all his five senses in perfect shape will now have—not the pleasure but the sadness of disclosing to you tonight a little corner of reality.

Let me warn you, in all humility, that nothing is made up. Angels, shadows, voices, snow lyres, and dreams *do* exist and fly among you—real as any lust, the coins in your pocket or the latest cancer in the lovely woman's breast or the salesman's tired lip.

You come to the theatre with the express desire to be entertained, and you have directors you pay to do it, and rightly so, but today you've a poet who will shut you in because he desires and aspires to touch your hearts, showing the things you don't want to see and shouting the simplest truths you don't want to hear.

And why? If you believe in God, and I do, why are you so afraid of death? And if you believe you're going to die, why such cruelty, such indifference to the terrible suffering of your fellow human beings?

Ha! You'll say this is a sermon. All right. But is a sermon so awful? Most of you listening to me once ran out of the house, slamming the door behind you on a mother or father who'd been scolding you for your own good, and now, at this moment, you'd give everything you have, including both eyes, to go back and hear their sweet vanished voices. The same thing applies here and now. But it's hard to face reality. And to show it, even harder. It's preaching in the desert. But never mind.

Anyhow, you city folks, living with the saddest and skimpiest fantasies—all you ever do is look for ways *not* to get involved. When the wind blows you play the pianola so you won't hear what it's saying. To avoid the heavy torrent of tears around us you hang lace curtains on your windows. To sleep easy and muffle the perennial buzz of conscience you create poorhouses.

A sermon, is it? All right, a sermon! Why should we go to the theatre to see what happens to others and not what's happening to us? The spectator feels safe because he knows the play's not going to be about himself; but how great it would be if he were suddenly called onstage and made to speak, and the sunlight of the stage burned through that trapped-looking white mask of his!

Reality is where the director begins because he doesn't want you feeling you're in the theatre but out there in the street. And that's why he's not after making poetry, balanced speeches, literature—he'd rather plant a little lesson in your hearts. That's what he's a poet for, though very modestly. Anyone can do the same. The director knows how to write poems, and I think he does well enough. He's a good theatre man too, but yesterday he told me all art is half artifice, and that's begun to bother him because he had no intention of dragging in the sweet smell of white lilies or some braided column clouded with golden doves. *(Claps his hands)* Would someone please bring me a cup of coffee? *(A curtain falls, depicting houses and trash. Pause.)* Very strong. *(He sits down. Violins are heard.)* The smell of white lilies isn't so unpleasant, but I prefer the smell of the sea. I could say the sea is full of the smell of sirens' breasts and a thousand other things, but the sea doesn't care and doesn't listen. It keeps calling to the sea-coasts, hoping for some freshly drowned corpses. That's what matters to people. But how could you bring the smell of the sea into a theatre or flood the orchestra with stars?

MALE SPECTATOR 1 *(from the orchestra):* Tear off the roof.

DIRECTOR: Don't interrupt me!

MALE SPECTATOR 1: I've got a right to. I paid admission.

DIRECTOR: Paying admission gives you no right to interrupt the actor, much less judge the work.

MALE SPECTATOR 1: It certainly does!

DIRECTOR: Like it or not, applaud it or not, but never pass judgment.

MALE SPECTATOR 1: The only law of the theatre is the judgment of the audience.

(Enter a man running, dressed in red tights. He is wearing a wolf's head. He leaps twice and falls down, stage-center.)

DIRECTOR: Who's this? See, you've hurt yourself. Now don't come around here again! I say it's strictly forbidden.

VOICE *(offstage):* Lorenzo, Lorenzo, my love!

(The wolf leaves, lit up and followed by a spotlight.)

MALE SPECTATOR 1: That's just awful!

DIRECTOR: Be good enough to keep still!

MALE SPECTATOR 1: I've paid to see theatre.

DIRECTOR: Theatre? What's that? We're not in any theatre here.

MALE SPECTATOR 1: We're not?

DIRECTOR *(violently):* No, sir. The fact is you're scared. You sense, because you know me, that I want to tear the walls down so we can hear people outside murder, cry, snore with their rotten bellies full, people who don't even know the theatre exists, and that's why you're scared. But go ahead and leave. At home you've got the lie waiting for you—you've got the tea, the radio, and the wife who while she's making love is thinking of the soccer player who lives in the small hotel across the street.

MALE SPECTATOR 1: If we weren't where we are I'd go up there and knock you down.

DIRECTOR: I'd turn the other cheek. Coward.

SERVANT *(entering):* Your coffee.

MALE SPECTATOR 1: I'm too close to reality to take you seriously.

DIRECTOR: Reality. Ha. So you know all about reality? Listen here. The wood for all our coffins—all of us here in this hall—has already been cut. Four caskets are waiting in the window for four of us creatures listening to me now, and maybe there's one—just maybe!—one that'll be filled before dawn, not much after you leave this delightful little place.

MALE SPECTATOR 1: I didn't come here to be preached at or to hear disagreeable stuff. Be glad you're in Spain, a country that's fond of death. In England they'd have hooted you offstage by now. I'm going. I thought I was in the theatre.

DIRECTOR: You're not in the theatre. Because they'll come and break down the doors. And so we'll all be saved. There's the terrible smell of lies in here, and actors in our plays say only what they're permitted to say aloud in front of frail young women, while stifling their real anguish. That's why I don't want actors but flesh-and-blood men and women, and anyone who'd rather not listen, let him plug up his ears.

MALE SPECTATOR 1: Let's go, honey. This chap's going to end up saying something abominable.

FEMALE SPECTATOR 1: I don't want to go. His line interests me.

DIRECTOR: You mean life interests you. Incredible life, which doesn't really exist in the theatre. A few days ago in this very spot I was able to stage for some friends, who were tear-proof, a real-life scene your own husband wouldn't believe. In a tiny room a woman has died of hunger. Her two starving children are playing with her hands, tenderly, as if with yellow loaves of bread. When night comes the children uncover the dead woman's breasts and fall asleep on them, as they eat a can of shoe polish.

MALE SPECTATOR 1: That's a pack of lies!

DIRECTOR: That man there knows I'm telling the truth precisely.

MALE SPECTATOR 1: Let's go, I tell you.

FEMALE SPECTATOR 1: Don't get so upset. In the theatre it's all make-believe.

DIRECTOR: It's not make-believe, it's the truth!

FEMALE SPECTATOR 1: Well, if it's the truth, let's go. How horrible, how disagreeable!

MALE SPECTATOR 1 (to the USHER, leaving): Go get us a taxi!

FEMALE SPECTATOR 1: How could you permit such things to be said to my face? It was all true! How come they weren't jailed immediately?

MALE SPECTATOR 1: Go on! I just knew you'd get sick over it. (Exit)

YOUTH (wearing a tuxedo, from a box): At this rate, you'll have no audience left.

DIRECTOR: Ah, was that you over there?

YOUTH: Yes, your experience interests me a good deal.

VOICE (offstage): Lorenzo! Lorenzo darling!

DIRECTOR: Excuse me. *(going over to the* SERVANT *who is holding the cup of coffee)*

YOUTH: I don't think these people will let you get away with it. Theatre is so wonderful! What will they do with the silver goblets, the ermine cloaks...? That voice that just rang out a second time has moved me more than any one real and about to die...

DIRECTOR: All that's already disappeared from the theatre. *(to the* SERVANT*)* How come you bring so little coffee and it tastes so vile?

SERVANT: I couldn't help it—it spilled. It was all dark and I bumped into some fishermen who were singing, carrying lead fish on their heads. Then they threw some gauze over me, the gauze was full of flies, and an old man said it was the mist. I'm not used to such things and I got scared.

DIRECTOR: Scared of stage scenery?

SERVANT: It's light in my cafe.

DIRECTOR: And there you're not afraid.

SERVANT: No, sir.

DIRECTOR: Many drunks go there?

SERVANT: Yes.

DIRECTOR: And they talk?

SERVANT: It's all drunk talk. Yesterday they brought in some kid and a big turkey and made bets to see which would get drunk first. The kid they gave cognac and the turkey they gave anís with bits of tobacco. We laughed ourselves sick. The kid got drunk first and began hitting his head against the walls. They cut off the turkey's head with a straight razor. Then they ate it up.

YOUTH: You see? That's your reality. The kid would bawl buckets over any straight little love story. That's the scene that's missing. You're doomed to flop.

DIRECTOR: Why didn't you stop them?

SERVANT: I've got to be nice to the customers.

DIRECTOR: And you weren't scared?

SERVANT *(laughing):* How could I be scared of a kid and a turkey? When they were cutting off the head they still threw a glass of anís down its open beak. It lasted almost half an hour because the razor was dull.

DIRECTOR: Shut up!

SERVANT: Does that scare you? Did you ever go to the carnivals? Last year a drunk came by playing the violin. I still have to laugh just thinking about it. Do you know what his fiddle was? A crucified cat nailed head first on a washboard; the bow was a great bunch of brambles and when it was played against the little animal, the cat let out shrieks that became the music for two elegantly dressed women to dance to—one dressed as Pierrot, the other as Columbine.

YOUTH: Sing them any corny little love song, and watch them bawl their eyes out!

DIRECTOR: Would you leave me *alone!*

YOUTH: I'm just trying to warn you. Those who claim to know would call it barbarism, others aberrant behavior, and turn their backs on it all so they can sleep more soundly.

DIRECTOR: They've got to be waked up and have their eyes opened, whatever they think.

YOUTH: But why?

DIRECTOR: So they'll see.

YOUTH: And you can be sure that coming out of their dream, with the reins of their conventional conscience still slack, half of them will ask for that bunch of brambles so they can bear down delightedly on the crucified animal.

SERVANT: And they'd be doing what's right. Cats are dangerous. They scratch children and can't be trusted.

DIRECTOR *(to the* YOUTH*):* I'm not trying to correct anybody. All I want is to have people tell the truth. And this one lets it *all* out in public.

YOUTH: Partly.

DIRECTOR: Sure, because it's still only half lit up. You need spotlights so strong they'd burn and cut the heart out of the person telling lies. *(to the* SERVANT*)* You can go. (SERVANT *leaves)* No! *(looking to the left)* I told you not to come this way. I don't want to set eyes on you. I'm tired of lies.

SERVANT *(entering):* Sir.

DIRECTOR: What?

SERVANT: Would you please tell the stagehands to light a light?

DIRECTOR: What for?

SERVANT: So I can get out.

DIRECTOR: Follow the passageway to the left and to the back, raise the curtain there, cross the rehearsal room and up the stairs you'll find the street.

SERVANT: It's just that . . .

DIRECTOR: Come on, get going!

SERVANT: It's that I'm scared. I have to jump through the fog that's all over the floor and there are those two big birds up on the skylight.

DIRECTOR: Have them turn up the lights. It's nothing. You'll see. Just some bits of gauze and painted props.

SERVANT: Yes, yes. But they look real.

DIRECTOR: And what if they were?

SERVANT: Ah, if they were, then just by taking a shot at them . . .

YOUTH: Bravo, of course! (SERVANT *leaves. Three heavy blows are heard and a curtain falls. On it is painted an improbable palace.*)

PROMPTER (*entering*): Director, sir, are you coming to the rehearsal?

DIRECTOR: No. What's being rehearsed?

PROMPTER: *A Midsummer Night's Dream.*

DIRECTOR: People can weep over *Othello* and laugh over *The Taming of the Shrew,* but they don't understand *A Midsummer Night's Dream,* and they laugh at it. It's just as well they don't understand it. Do you know the plot?

PROMPTER: I'm a prompter. I can't explain it too well.

DIRECTOR: It's a gloomy story.

PROMPTER: It makes *me* quite happy.

DIRECTOR: Well, it's not happy. The whole play tries to show that love, on whatever level, is an accident and has nothing to do with us at all. People keep sleeping, Puck, the little fairy, comes and makes them smell a flower; they wake and fall in love with the first person who comes along, even though they were in love with someone else before they fell asleep. So Titania, queen of the fairies, falls in love with a peasant wearing an ass's head. It's a terrible truth, but a destructive truth can lead to suicide and now more than ever the world needs consoling truths, truths to build from. One shouldn't think of oneself but of others. I'm not going back to the rehearsal.

PROMPTER: How do we imitate the breeze that blows in the forest scenes?

DIRECTOR: Any way you wish. Hum with your mouth closed. But leave me alone. Today's the last day I'll ever set foot in a theatre.

ACTRESS *(enters dressed as Titania):* Lorenzo, Lorenzo! Aren't you coming? I can't work without you. If I don't see the sunset, which I so much adore, and if I don't run barefoot through the high grass, it's simply to follow after you and be with you in these lower depths.

DIRECTOR *(mordantly):* Where did you learn that sentence? What play are you quoting from?

ACTRESS: None at all. I speak it for the first time.

DIRECTOR: You lie. If that body of yours really belonged to you, I'd whip you to see if you were telling the truth.

ACTRESS: Lorenzo.

DIRECTOR: You imagine that because you're dressed as Titania you'll intoxicate me, and you're mistaken. Tomorrow you'll be dressed as a beggar, a fine lady, and the next day you'll be the serpent in a fable by some tricky poet.

ACTRESS: I only know I love you. I'd like you to whip me so you'll see my skin grow rosy. I want you to pierce me in the breast so you'll see a thread of blood spurt out. Ha ha. And if you like blood you'll drink mine and give me a little.

DIRECTOR: Liar.

ACTRESS: Of course it's a lie! *(embracing him)* Here I am, myself alone, and yet in each of your eyes you see me differently, and very small. If snow flies from fire, how can you bear those cold teeth between the hot coals of your lips? It's all a lie! I'd love you to be one of those gray horses that go out at dawn looking for fillies in the dark stables. No, no.

DIRECTOR: Leave me alone!

ACTRESS: Ha ha. You're a bear. Don't you believe anything I tell you? Try crushing me and watch me go into my death throes against your hairy chest. Till yesterday I loved soft silky skin. Now I love horsehair, filthy ghettos, and a shepherd's hovel.

DIRECTOR: Don't think you're coming along with me to indulge those little yens of yours. I won't oblige you. I'm really going off to escape you, your company, your fickleness.

ACTRESS: Is it because I can't be one of those ugly women you're looking for, some lady leper, to keep you company? Yes. You belong to me. Ah, if you only could watch me enjoy dying with you, in a hospital.

DIRECTOR: You'd never tell me the truth.

ACTRESS: Nor anyone. But I would sing you the most beautiful lie. Me—I like the truth too, for a moment, no longer. Truth is ugly, and if I tell it they'll throw me out of the theatre. I know the urge to turn to the audience, in the most lyrical scene, and suddenly fling them some obscenity, the filthiest kind. Ha ha. But I love my emeralds and they'd take them away from me.

DIRECTOR *(furious):* Get out of here, get out!

ACTRESS: Ah, so you're going to whip me after all? I know you don't like Titania. She's a fairy and fairies don't exist. But Lady Macbeth is something else. *(She takes off her white wig and reveals a black one. She discards her large black cape and appears in a fiery red dress. The back curtain rises on a gloomy stone cloister with fantastic trees.)* Yes, Lady Macbeth exists, and what's more, now you're afraid of me. *(The light changes slowly into blue moonlight)* Because I'm beautiful, because I live forever, because I'm fed up with blood. Fed up with real blood! Through the centuries over three thousand boys have died, burnt up by my stare. Boys who once were alive and whom I saw through their agonies of passion between the bedsheets.

DIRECTOR: What was the book you got that paragraph out of? You're nothing but an actress, a contemptible actress!

ACTRESS: A comedienne, who's dying for you, Lorenzo! Who begs you not to abandon her.

DIRECTOR *(shouting):* Give us some light here, please, and raise the curtains.

ACTRESS: That's it. Red light, red light to see these bloody hands of mine. They've turned on the moonlight and now I want to do the last scene for you. *(Red light)*

DIRECTOR *(to the electricians):* Didn't you hear me?

ACTRESS: Silence! You've got to take me by force. Blood spilt on the ground turns to mud. What do I care if soldiers are slain? But if it spilt on a bowl of hyacinths, it turns into the richest tasting wine. *(shots are heard)*

DIRECTOR: What's going on? Turn all the lights on. Light up the lobby! *(NICK BOTTOM crosses the stage with an ass's head in his hand)*

NICK BOTTOM: It's terrible! Come this way! We'll be safe inside!

(Sounds of shots come closer)

FEMALE SPECTATOR 2 *(seated in the middle of the orchestra):* Let's go. I'm worried about the children at home alone.

MALE SPECTATOR 1: The military must have taken over the streets, and won't let anyone through.

PROMPTER *(on the stage):* It seems they're getting closer. The whole lobby is full of people.

VOICE: Long live the Revolution! *(The ACTRESS quickly dons a raincoat and hides her hair under a gray felt hat)*

ACTRESS: Shut the doors, shut them!

DIRECTOR: Open them! The theatre belongs to everyone! This is the people's school!

ACTRESS: No, let nobody in. They'll break the real dishes, the fake books, the delicate glass moon. They'll spill the marvelous elixirs preserved through the centuries and they'll destroy the rainmaking machine!

DIRECTOR: Let them break it all!

ACTRESS: They'll leave your stage in utter ruins, my darling.

DIRECTOR *(to the PROMPTER):* I've said I want the doors left open. I won't have real blood spilled near the walls of lies.

PROMPTER: Very well. Whatever you say. But what about the economics? What's to be done about the economics of the theatre?

DIRECTOR *(furious):* What do you mean, the economics?

PROMPTER: It's a mystery all sensible people respect and I have faith in it.

DIRECTOR: To hell with the economics! Do you hear? Do you hear me?

PROMPTER *(trembling):* Yes, but please, get me some cotton to stuff in my ears!

DIRECTOR: That's the sound of real blood!

ACTRESS: Don't stick your head out, Lorenzo! A stray bullet may kill you!

DIRECTOR *(sarcastically):* Where's Lady Macbeth now?

ACTRESS: Lady Macbeth cannot speak while volleys of gunfire mow down the roses in the gardens.

MAN DRESSED IN BLACK *(entering):* You're quite right. Gunpowder kills poetry.

DIRECTOR: Or saves it!

MAN DRESSED IN BLACK: An iron fist! A good iron fist! Let's make one giant rose out of rebels' heads! Let's decorate the façades and the lampposts, the thousand-year-old porticos, with garlands made of the tongues that want to destroy the status quo.

(Enter onstage a WOODSMAN with a totally white face, a load of wood on his back, and a little lamp in hand)

WOODSMAN: It looks like the rebels are beating a retreat.

MAN DRESSED IN BLACK: That's it! They've got to be beaten!

DIRECTOR: Who are you?

MAN DRESSED IN BLACK: Myself. The owner of the theatre. An iron fist! In our time the good, the true, and the beautiful must proceed with rifle in hand *(exit).*

WOODSMAN: Very well put!

DIRECTOR: Why do you say that? How much do you earn?

WOODSMAN: A small pittance. Enough to feed me. But all I ever want is to be left in peace to play my part.

Spikenard may be star or snowflake,
Night sky some tattered draperies.
Let locusts sing or wild winds howl.
What counts is the dreams in your eyes.

DIRECTOR: What part are you playing?

WOODSMAN: I am Shakespeare's moon.

DIRECTOR: Not *here* you are!

WOODSMAN: Forever. Just try and bury me and you'll see how fast I get out! *(Two cannon shots are heard)*

PROMPTER *(enters):* The armed forces are now fighting in the main square.

(Leaves. Enter MALE *and* FEMALE SPECTATORS 2, *who were previously in the audience)*

FEMALE SPECTATOR 2: Enrique, it's the Revolution. The Revolution!

MALE SPECTATOR 2: Any chance of the bullets coming my way?

WOODSMAN: None at all, but you'll be safer over there. What's bad is if the airplanes come. But that's nothing to me, in the end. I have a speech that expresses it all.

> For my October moon, the air
> Is neither arrow, bird, nor sigh.
> As men will sleep, so grasses die.
> Alive is this: my ring of silver,
> Love underwater—dwell there forever!
> Damp forget-me-nots, turn cold.
> Roofs may all be stained with blood,
> But stain shining garments? Never!

(weeps) It's such a pretty song, it may be they'll never let me sing it again!

FEMALE SPECTATOR 2: What's he saying?

NICK BOTTOM *(entering):* I saw four airplanes approaching.

FEMALE SPECTATOR 2: My children! My poor children! My house is sure to be stormed, and as the children are alone with the governess and servants, they'll all be killed!

VOICE *(from the front row of the top gallery):* The workers never did anything like that, nor will they ever!

MALE SPECTATOR 2 *(to the audience):* They have *so* done it!

DIRECTOR *(to the* MALE SPECTATOR*):* You're lying!

MALE SPECTATOR 2: In some revolution a few years back they tore out the eyes of three hundred children, some of them infants.

DIRECTOR: Who told you this? What scoundrel has muddied his tongue with such a nightmare! Tell me!

MALE SPECTATOR 2: Moderate your tone of voice and speak with the customary propriety of a gentleman.

DIRECTOR: I'm no gentleman, nor care to be one. I'm on my last legs searching for the truth of God.

MALE SPECTATOR 2: Horsefeathers!

FEMALE SPECTATOR 2 *(frightened and grabbing her husband):* Enrique, oh Enrique!

MALE SPECTATOR 2: I know all about it. A newspaper friend of mine—a great journalist—was there when it happened. And to prove it he carried around in a small lacquered box two living blue eyes which he showed everybody.

PROMPTER *(entering):* The planes are beginning the bombardment.

FEMALE SPECTATOR 2: My sons, oh my little boys! *(to* DIRECTOR*)* Especially the smaller one, he can't live without me. He's a blond boy, and comes in every morning singing an English song to waken me. He cannot live without me!

MALE SPECTATOR 2: At night he'll miss her the most, because, without any thought of her social rank, she undresses him herself!

FEMALE SPECTATOR 2: And they'll be murdered, my God, they'll be murdered!

STAGEHAND *(coming out of the shadows):* Don't be afraid, señora. I'll go myself. I'll dodge the bullets and tell them you're safe and sound.

DIRECTOR: You're going out?

STAGEHAND: Yes!

DIRECTOR: I'll go up and watch through the skylight window.

ACTRESS *(behind):* Lorenzo, don't show yourself. Keep your splendid talent out of danger. *(Exit backstage)*

STAGEHAND: If I find there's no danger, I'll bring them back to you. You are parents and I understand your anxiety. If this continues, belowstage is the best spot in the city.

FEMALE SPECTATOR 2: Yes, go now! Go.

STAGEHAND *(leaving):* I'll do my best.

MALE SPECTATOR 2: Who is that man?

WOODSMAN: A stagehand!

MALE SPECTATOR 2: What's his name?

WOODSMAN: His comrades here call him Crazy Bakúnin.

FEMALE SPECTATOR 2: We've got to help him. I'd give him everything I have. Why are you asking for his name?

MALE SPECTATOR 2: Just because. *(aside)* And to denounce him later. *(writes in a little notebook)*

(The aerial bombardment is heard. People begin running to the walls. The DIRECTOR *climbs up a stairway out of sight)*

VOICE *(from the gallery):* Dirty scoundrel!

MALE SPECTATOR 2: You're up there in the shadows but I'll light up the dark and drag you off in chains. I belong to the army of the Lord, and I count on his support. When I die I shall see Him in all His glory and He will love me. My God is unforgiving. He is the God of the armies. To Him you surrender by force since there's no other truth.

WOODSMAN: Stick close to the wall and protect yourself! It's a total bombardment!

MALE SPECTATOR 2: I'm not afraid. God is with me.

VOICE: I don't believe in God!

MALE SPECTATOR 2: I know that, but this is the way we pull out the weeds.

(He takes out a small flashlight and shines it towards the gallery, which stays lit up.)

WORKER *(dressed in overalls, raising his arms):* Comrades!

(The whole theatre lights up.)

MALE SPECTATOR 2 *(coldly):* Ah, that's my fellow! *(He draws a pistol and fires. The* WORKER *cries out and falls)*

FIRST WOMAN: You've killed him!

SECOND WOMAN: Assassin, assassin!

MALE SPECTATOR 2: Get the ushers here to remove those who interfere with the performance! *(He clicks off his flashlight and the whole theatre darkens again and stays dark)* Good hunting! God will reward me. Bless the Lord in his most Holy vengeance. The Lord is One!

YOUTH *(from the audience, breaking into peals of laughter):* The Lord is One, and of course Mohammed is his Prophet! Why don't you shoot me? Since the revolution is in full swing, nothing will happen to you.

MALE SPECTATOR 2: Where Jews and other shady characters are concerned, one must proceed with special caution.

YOUTH: I'm sorry. I'm not a Jew. I'm a Muslim.

MALE SPECTATOR 2: Doesn't the bombardment scare you?

YOUTH: Less than it does you. I'd sort of like to die and have a million mistresses. Women are expensive around here.

MALE SPECTATOR 2 (*looking both ways before speaking*): Terribly expensive, but the day will come, and I believe it's at hand, when we'll get them cheaply once again. My ancestors had them in pairs.

YOUTH: Happy days! I certainly congratulate you, seeing you're such a wonderful shot!

MALE SPECTATOR 2: My teacher was a German lieutenant who'd been through all the African wars. His only target was man. To kill a bird filled him with disgust.

YOUTH (*lowering his voice*): It was a magnificent hit. Was it in the heart!

MALE SPECTATOR 2: In the heart would have made him leap up, and he fell backwards without opening his mouth. It was in the forehead, dead center. (*A thunderous noise of bombs fills the stage.*)

FEMALE SPECTATOR 2: Enrique, Enrique. Come here, quickly, please.

MALE SPECTATOR 2: There's really no danger! (*He goes to his wife. The bombardment increases. Lights of all sorts flash across the stage. Backstage a group of people wearing the costumes of sylphs and fairies are carrying a wounded worker*)

FAIRY: He fell from the skylight.

SYLPH: Pea Blossom, be careful to support his head.

WORKER (*dying*): Viva la revolución!

FAIRY: Let's carry him to the dressing room.

SYLPH: Get me a handkerchief!

FAIRY: Right away, quickly! (*they leave*)

FEMALE SPECTATOR 2: My sons, my sons!

ACTRESS: I'm sick of hearing that cry uttered so poorly. I can't stand it. In her voice there's a false note that won't ever succeed in moving a soul. Not like that—like this: My sons, oh my sons! My darling little children! Did you hear that? My darling little children! And with the hands thrust forward—so—making them tremble, as if they were two leaves caught in a fevered breeze.

STAGEHAND (*entering*): The people have broken in the doors! (MALE SPECTATOR 2 *makes a motion to draw his pistol, his wife restrains him*)

DIRECTOR (*leaving*): Here, right here! Let the truth be told on all the old stages. Plunge daggers into the old monopolists of your daily bread and olive oil. Let the rain drench the backdrops and wash away all the old scenery.

VOICE: Fire!

VOICE *(farther off):* Fire!

DIRECTOR *(going off):* And fire!

   (The theatre lights all go red)

ACTRESS *(entering) (raising her voice):* Lorenzo! *(lowers it, trembling)* Lorenzo!

Curtain

DIVAN POEMS

(Diván del Tamarit)

Twelve Gacelas

I

GACELA OF LOVE UNFORESEEN

No one understood the perfume
of your belly's dark magnolia.
No one knew you tormenting
love's hummingbird between your teeth.

A thousand Persian ponies fell asleep
in the moonlit plaza of your forehead
as four nights through I hugged
your waist, snow's enemy.

Between plaster and jasmines your glance
was a pale seed-branch.
I searched my heart to give you
the ivory letters saying *always,*

Always, always: garden of my agony,
your body eluding me forever,
the blood of your veins in my mouth,
your mouth's light gone out for my death.

II

GACELA OF THE TERRIBLE PRESENCE

I want water left blind to its sources.
I want wind left blind to the valleys.

I want night deprived of its eyes
and my heart of its flower of gold.

Let oxen speak with the huge leaves
and earthworms die of the darkness.

Let teeth in the skull glitter and shine
and the yellows spread through the silk.

I can watch wounded night in its duel,
wrestling and writhing with noon.

I can stand a poison-green sunset
and the ruined archways of suffering time.

But don't show your nakedness, clean
as black cactus alive in the reeds.

Let me go on fearing dark planets
but don't show me your glistening waist.

III

GACELA OF DESPERATE LOVE

Night doesn't want to fall—
only to keep you from coming
and me from going off.

But off I'll go anyway,
with a scorpion sun eating my brain.

But you will come anyway,
with a tongue burnt by salt rain.

Day docsn't want to break—
only to keep you from coming
and me from going off.

But off I'll go anyway,
lcaving toads my chewed-up carnation.

But you will come anyway,
through the slimy sewers of darkness.

Night won't fall and day won't break—
just so I'd die for you
and you would for me.

IV

GACELA OF LOVE THAT WON'T BE SEEN

Just hearing the bell toll
in the tower of Vela
I crowned you with verbena.

Granada a moon
drowned in ivy.

Just hearing the bell toll
in the tower of Vela
I tore up my garden in Cartagena.

Granada a rose-colored deer
in the weathervanes.

Just hearing the bell toll
in the tower of Vela
I burned in your body
not knowing yours from mine.

V

GACELA OF THE DEAD CHILD

Each afternoon in Granada,
a child dies each afternoon.
Each afternoon the water sits down
to chat with its companions.

The dead wear mossy wings.
One wind clear and one cloudy
are two pheasants in flight through the towers,
and the day is a wounded boy.

When I found you in the wine caverns
not a flicker of larks remained in the sky,
not the crumb of a cloud lay overground
when you drowned in the river.

A giant of water sprawled over the hills,
the valley tumbling with lilies and dogs.
Through my hands' violet shadow your body
dead on the bank, was an archangel, cold.

VI

GACELA OF THE BITTER ROOT

There is a bitter root
and the world with a thousand terraces.

The tiniest hand of all
won't soften the door of water.

Where are you going, where, oh where?
There's a sky with a thousand windows
—battle of angry bees—
and there's a bitter root.

Bitter.

The ache in the sole of your foot
aches inside your cheeks
and aches in the night's wet trunk
recently lopped off.

O love, my enemy,
bite your bitter root!

VII

GACELA OF LOVE'S MEMORY

Don't carry your memory off.
Leave it alone in my heart,

trembling white cherry
in martyred January.

A wall of bad dreams
cuts me off from the dead.

To a heart of plaster
I offer a fresh lily's pain.

All night in the garden
my eyes like two dogs.

All night eating
poisoned quince fruit.

At times the wind
is a tulip of fright,

ailing tulip,
winter dawn.

A wall of bad dreams
cuts me off from the dead.

Grass quietly covers
your body's gray valley.

At the arch where we met
the hemlock is growing.

But leave your memory whole,
leave it alone in my heart.

VIII

GACELA OF DARK DEATH

I want to sleep the dream of apples
and leave the tumult of cemeteries.
I want to sleep the dream of that child
eager to cut his heart on the high seas.

I don't want to be told again that the dead
don't lose their blood,
that the rotting mouth still begs for water.
I don't want to know of martyrs to the grass
nor of the moon's snake mouth
that goes to work before dawn.

I want to sleep a little,
a while, a minute, a century,
but let them know that I haven't died,
that there's a stable of gold in my lips,
that I'm the West wind's little friend
and the huge shadow of my tears.

Cover me with a veil at dawn, the dawn
that will hurl fistfuls of ants at me,
and drench my shoes with hard water
to let the scorpion's claws slide there.

Because I want to sleep the dream of apples
to learn a lament to cleanse me of earth,
because I want to live with that dark child
eager to cut his heart on the high seas.

IX

GACELA OF MIRACULOUS LOVE

In all the plaster
of blighted fields
you were love's reed, dewy jasmine.

In south wind and flame
of blighted skies
you were snow, stirring my heart.

Skies and fields
knotted chains in my hands.

Fields and skies
whipped my body's wounds.

X

GACELA OF THE ESCAPE

I have often lost myself in the sea,
ears full of newly cut flowers,
tongue full of love and agony.
I have often lost myself in the sea,
as I lose myself in the heart of some children.

There's no one who on kissing another fails
to feel the smile of faceless people,
nor one who on touching a newborn child
forgets the horse's motionless skull.

Because roses search the forehead
for a stiff landscape of bone,
and men's hands have no other purpose
than to imitate underground roots.

As I lose myself in the heart of some children
I have often lost myself in the sea.
Mindless of water I go looking
for a dying of light to consume me.

XI

GACELA OF LOVE ONE HUNDRED YEARS OLD

Up the street go
the four gallants.

ay, ay, ay, ay.

Down the street three
gallants stroll by.

ay, ay, ay.

They tighten their waists,
those two gallants.

ay, ay.

See one gallant turn his face
flush with the wind!

Ay.

Through the myrtles
no one strolls by.

XII

GACELA OF THE MARKET IN THE MORNING

Through Elvira's arch
I must see you go by,
to find out your name
and begin to cry.

What gray moon at nine
drew the blood from your cheek?
Who takes in the seed
of your flare-up in snow?
What small cactus needle
destroys your crystal?

Through Elvira's arch
I must see you go by,
to drink in your eyes
and begin to cry.

What shouts in the market
you raise up against me!
Like cast-off carnations
on mountains of wheat!
How distant I am when near you,
how close when you're gone!

Through Elvira's arch
I must see you go by,
to drink in your eyes
and begin to cry.

Nine Casidas

I

CASIDA OF THE BOY WOUNDED BY WATER

I want to go down to the well,
I want to go up the walls of Granada
to look at his heart transfixed
by the dark drill of the waters.

The wounded boy was groaning
under his crown of frost.
Pools, cisterns, fountains
raised their swords in the air.
Ah, what a fury of love with its wounding edge,
what murmurs that night, what a white death!
Ah, what deserts of light went flooding
the sandpits of dawn!
The boy was alone,
the city asleep in his throat.
Out of his dreams a water spout rose
to ward off the hungry algae.
The boy and his agony, face to face,
were two green rains enlaced,
the boy stretched out on the ground
with his agony bent over.

I want to go down to the well,
I want to die my own death, by mouthfuls,
I want to stuff my heart with moss,
to look at the boy wounded by water.

II

CASIDA OF THE LAMENT

I have shut my balcony tight
for I cannot stand the lament,
but behind gray walls one hears
nothing but the lament.

Here very few angels may sing,
and very few dogs may bark,
a thousand violins
fit the palm of my hand.

But the lament is a dog, immense,
the lament is an angel, immense,
the lament's an immense violin,
tears stifle the wind, and one hears
nothing but the lament.

III

CASIDA OF THE BRANCHES

Through the orchards of the Tamarit
dogs of lead have come,
expecting the branches to fall,
the branches to break by themselves.

In the Tamarit an apple tree
has an apple full of sobs.
A nightingale cuts off its sighs
and a pheasant routs them in dust.

But the branches themselves are happy,
the branches are just like us,
not thinking of rain they have fallen asleep
like trees, all of a sudden.

Two valleys with water up to their knees
were waiting for autumn.
Twilight came in like an elephant,
knocking branches and tree trunks around.

Through the orchard of the Tamarit
are many children with shrouded faces,
expecting my branches to fall,
my branches to break by themselves.

IV

CASIDA OF THE WOMAN RECLINING

Seeing you naked brings back the earth,
smooth earth, cleared of horses.
Earth without reeds, pure form shut
on the future: confine of silver.

Seeing you naked brings back the rain
anxious to find a frail form
or the huge-faced sea feverishly
seeking the light on its cheek.

Blood will resound through the bedrooms
and come with a flashing of swords,
but you'll never find the heart of the toad
or know where the violet lies hidden.

Your belly is a battle of roots,
your lips an unshapened dawn.
Under the bed's warm roses dead men
whimper, waiting their turn.

V

CASIDA OF THE DREAM OUT-OF-DOORS

Flowery jasmine, beheaded bull.
Endless pavement. Map. Hall. Harp and dawn.
The girl dreams of a jasmine bull
and the bull is a bleeding twilight roaring.

If the sky were a very small boy,
jasmines would be half-lit, half dark night,
and the bull a blue bullfighterless ring
with a heart at the foot of a column.

But the sky is an elephant,
the jasmine a bloodless water,
and the girl is a branch at night
over the huge dark pavement.

Between the bull and the jasmine
ivory hooks or people asleep.
In the jasmine an elephant, clouds,
and in the bull the girl's skeleton.

VI

CASIDA OF THE IMPOSSIBLE HAND

I want no more than a hand,
a wounded hand, if possible.
I want no more than a hand,
though I spend a thousand sleepless nights.

Let it be a lily white as lime,
let it be a dove fastened to my heart,
let it be my angel who strictly forbids
the moon to shine the night I disappear.

I want no more than a hand
for the daily unguents and white sheet of my agony.
I want no more than that hand
to be for me a wing toward death.

All the rest goes by.
A blush now nameless, perpetual star.
The rest is something else: a sad wind
through the leaves flurrying past.

VII

CASIDA OF THE ROSE

The rose
did not seek the dawn:
almost eternal on its branch,
it looked for something else.

The rose
did not seek to hide or know:
confine of flesh and dream,
it looked for something else.

The rose
did not seek the rose:
immobile through the sky,
it looked for something else.

VIII

CASIDA OF THE GOLDEN GIRL

The golden girl
was bathing in the water
when the water turned golden.

Shadowy branches
and the algae made her shudder,
and the nightingale was singing
for the girl in white.

Bright night came on,
streaked with cloudy silver,
and bald mountains
under the dusky breeze.

The girl was wet
and white in water,
and the water all ablaze.

Up rose the spotless dawn
with a thousand cowy faces,
with frozen garlands
still and shrouded.

The girl, all tears,
bathed herself in flames,
and the nightingale was weeping
in its burnt-black wings.

The golden girl
was a white heron
and the water had turned her golden.

IX

CASIDA OF THE DARK DOVES

Through the laurel branches
I saw two dark doves.
The sun was one,
the other was the moon.
Dear neighbors, I said,
where is my tomb?
In my tail, said the sun.
In my throat, said the moon.
And I who was walking around
with the earth at my waist,
saw two snow eagles
and a girl undressed.
One was the other
and the girl neither one.
Dear eagles, I said,
where is my tomb?
In my tail, said the sun.
In my throat, said the moon.
Through the laurel branches
I saw two doves undressed.
One was the other
and both neither one.

OTHER POEMS

FOR THE DEATH OF
JOSÉ DE CIRIA Y ESCALANTE

Who'll say I saw you, and when was it?
In this sorrow of lit penumbra
two voices resound, clock and wind,
as dawn without you floats over.

A delirium of ash-red spikenard
invades your delicate head.
Man! Passion! Sorrow of light! Memento!
The full moon returns: heart of nothingness.

The full moon returns: with my own hand
I'll hurl your apple over the river
crowded with red summer fishes.

And you, there above, green and cold,
forget yourself!—and forget this vain world,
delicate Giocondo, my friend.

YOUR CHILDHOOD IN MENTON

"Yes, your childhood now
a legend of fountains."
                    Jorge Guillén

Yes, your childhood now a legend of fountains.
The train, and the woman who fills the sky.
Your evasive solitude in hotels
and your pure mask of another sign.
It is the sea's childhood and the silence
where wisdom's glasses all are shattered.
It is your inert ignorance of where
my torso lay, bound by fire.
Man of Apollo, I gave you love's pattern,
the frenzied nightingale's lament.
But, pasture of ruins, you kept lean
for brief and indecisive dreams.
Thought of what was confronted, yesterday's light,
tokens and traces of chance.
Your restless waist of sand
favors only tracks that don't ascend.
But I must search all corners
for your tepid soul without you, which doesn't understand you
with my thwarted Apollonian sorrow
that broke through the mask you wear.
There, lion, there, heavenly fury,
I'll let you graze on my cheeks;
there, blue horse of my madness,
pulse of nebula and minute hand,
I'll search the stones for scorpions
and your childlike mother's clothes,
midnight lament and ragged cloth
that tore the moon out of the dead man's brow.
Yes, your childhood now a legend of fountains.
Soul a stranger to my veins' emptiness,
I'll search for you rootless and small.
Eternal love, love, love that never was!
Oh, yes! I love. Love, love! Leave me.

Don't let them gag me, they who seek
the wheat of Saturn through the snow,
who castrate creatures in the sky,
clinic and wilderness of anatomy.
Love, love, love. Childhood of the sea.
Your tepid soul without you which doesn't understand you.
Love, love, a flight of deer
through the endless heart of whiteness.
And your childhood, love, your childhood.
The train, and the woman who fills the sky.
Not you or I, not the wind or the leaves.
Yes, your childhood now a legend of fountains.

SUICIDE

(Maybe because he didn't know his geometry.)

One day at ten o'clock
the boy forgot.

His heart was filling up
with broken wings and paper flowers.

He noticed in his mouth
just one small word was left.

As he removed his gloves, a fine
thin ash fell from his hands.

From the balcony he saw a tower.
He felt himself both balcony and tower.

He saw of course how in its frame
the stopped clock observed him.

He saw his shadow stretched out still
on the silken white divan.

And the boy, rigid, geometric,
broke the mirror with an axe.

As it broke, a thick stream of shadow
flooded his chimeric chamber.

THE SPINSTER AT MASS

Beneath the Moses of the incense,
drowsing.

Bull eyes observe you.
Your rosary raining.

In that dress of silk so dense,
never stir, Virginia.

Give the black melons of your breasts
to the murmur of the mass.

NIGHT SONG OF THE ANDALUSIAN SAILORS

What a fine little road
to Gibraltar from Cádiz.
The sea recognizes my steps
by my sighs.

Ah, maid, maid,
so many boats in Malaga's harbor!

To Seville from Cádiz
what stretches of lemon trees!
The lemon tree recognizes me
by my sighs

Ay maid, maid,
so many boats in Malaga's harbor!

From Seville to Carmona
not a knife can be found.
The half moon cuts
and wounds the air that goes by.

Ah, lad, lad,
how the waves carry my horse over!

By the barren salt pits
I forgot you, my love.
Let him who needs a heart
beg my forgetfulness.

Ah, lad, lad,
how the waves carry my horse over!

Cádiz, never come near this place
or the sea will cover you.
Seville, stand on your toes
or the river will drown you.

Ah, maid, ah lad,
what a fine little road!
So many boats in the harbor,
and in the square, how cold!

SONG OF THE RIDER *(1860)*

In the black moon
of the highwaymen
spurs are jingling.

Black horse,
where are you carrying
your dead rider?

The hard spurs
of the motionless bandit
who lost his reins.

Cold horse,
what a flowery scent
of the knife!

In the black moon
the sides of the Sierra Morena
are bleeding.

Black horse,
where are you carrying
your dead rider?

Cold horse,
what a flowery scent
of the knife!

In the black moon
a shriek—and the long
horn of the bonfire.

Black horse,
where are you carrying
your dead rider?

SONG OF SMALL DEATH

Field alive with moons
and blood underground.
Field of old blood.

Yesterday's light and tomorrow's.
Sky with grass alive.
Light and night of sand.

I stumbled once on death.
Field alive with earth.
A small death.

Dog on the roof.
Only my left hand ran through
hills and hills of dead flowers.

Ashen cathedral.
Light and night of sand.
A small death.

Death and I, a man.
A man alone, and she,
a small death.

Field alive with moons.
Snow rattles and trembles outside
behind the door.

A man. What else? That's all.
A man alone and she.
Field, love, light, and sand.

Santa Lucía and San Lázaro

I arrived in the city at midnight. The frost danced on one foot. "A girl may be brunette, she may be blonde, but she must not be blind." This was what the landlord told a man brutally cut in two by a waist band. The eyes of a mule, dozing on the threshold, threatened me like two handfuls of jet.

"I want the best room you have."

"I have one."

"All right. Let's go."

The room had a mirror. I, half a comb in my pocket. "I like it." (I saw my "I like it" in the green mirror.) The landlord shut the door. Then, with my back turned to the little frozen field of mercury, I exclaimed again, "I like it." Below, the mule brayed. I mean, he opened the sunflower of his mouth.

There was nothing else to do but get into bed. I lay down, but was careful to leave the shutters open, for there is nothing more beautiful than the sight of one star surprised and framed in a window frame. One. The rest must be forgotten.

Tonight my sky is uneven and capricious. The stars congregate and vanish in the glass like imprints and pictures on a Japanese mat.

When I fell asleep, the exquisite minuet of farewell goodnights petered out down the streets.

With the rising sun, I turned my gray suit inside out to the silver of the humefied air. The spring day was like a hand fainted on a pillow. In the street the people were coming and going. Fruitsellers passed by, and deep-sea fish mongers.

Not a bird.

While playing my finger rings against the grillwork of the balcony, I looked for the city on a map and saw how it lay sleeping in yellow amid rich little veins of water—and the sea so far away!

Down in the courtyard, the landlord and his wife were singing a duet of hawthorn and violet. Their obscure voices, like two escaped moles, were stumbling against the walls unable to find the framed exit to the sky.

Before going into the streets to take my first walk, I went to greet them.

"Why did you say last night that a girl may be brunette or blonde, but she must not be blind?"

The landlord and his wife looked at each other strangely.

They looked at each other...mistaking themselves: like the child who brings a spoonful of soup to his eyes. Then they burst into tears.

I didn't know what to say and left hurriedly.

Over the door I read the inscription: *Inn of Santa Lucía.*

Santa Lucía was a beautiful virgin from Syracuse.

She has been portrayed with two magnificent ox eyes in a tray.

She suffered martyrdom under the consul Pascasiano, who had silver mustaches and howled like a mastiff.

Like all saints, she propounded and resolved delightful theorems on which the instruments of physics break their crystals.

She demonstrated in the public square, to the astonishment of the people, that a thousand men and fifty pairs of oxen could not contend with the luminous dove of the Holy Ghost. Her body, her enormous body, was made of compressed lead. Our Lord was seated, of course, with scepter and crown across her middle.

Santa Lucía was a tall girl with small breasts and opulent behind. Like all fierce women, her eyes were too large, virile, with a disagreeable dark light. She died in a bed of flames.

It was the busiest spot in the market-place and the shore of the day was filled with snails and ripe tomatoes. Before the miraculous façade of the cathedral, I understood perfectly how San Ramón Nonnato could cross the sea from the Balearic Islands to Barcelona seated on his cape, and how that most ancient sun of China grows furious and jumps like a cock over the musical towers made of dragon flesh.

People at the bars were drinking beer, and in the offices they were doing multiplications, while the + and × signs of the Jewish bank engaged in dark combat the sacred sign of the Cross, filled on the inside with saltpeter and snuffed-out tapers. The fat cathedral bell poured over the city a rain of little copper chimes which struck against the maddened trolleys and the agitated necks of horses. I had forgotten my Baedecker and my field glasses, and I began to see the city like one seeing the sea from the shore.

All the streets were full of optical shops. From the doorways gazed large megatheric eyes—terrible eyes looking out of an almond-shaped orbit which intensifies the human but which here hoped to pass its monstrosity off unnoticed, pretending to be the eyelids of every Tom, Dick, and Harry. Spectacles and smoked glasses sought the immense lopped-off hand of the glove shop, a poem in the air, that rang, bled and bubbled like the head of John the Baptist.

The happiness of the city stopped moving like the child who recently failed his exams. It had been happy, crowned with trills and grass trimmings, until but a few hours past, when the sadness which slackens electric cables and raises the portico tiles invaded the streets with its imperceptible murmur of a mirror's depth. I began to weep, because there is nothing more stirring than the new sadness upon merry things, still a little dense, proving that happiness can be seen straight through to its bottom, full of perforated coins.

The new-found sadness of curious little paper-bound books called "The Umbrella," "The Automobile" and "The Bicycle"; sadness of "Black and White" of 1910; sadness of the pointed lace-work fringe on the petticoat, and the sharp sadness of huge phonograph horns.

The optician's apprentices were cleaning glasses of all sizes with chamois skin and fine paper, making the sound of a snake crawling.

In the cathedral, they were offering a solemn novena to the human eyes of Santa Lucía. They glorified the exteriors of things: the cool clean beauty of the skin, the delight of graceful surfaces, and they sought succor against the dark physiologies of the body, against the fire at the center and the trickeries of night. And under the unembossed dome, they raised a sheet of purest glass, pierced by five golden reflectors from all directions. The world of grass opposed the world of minerals. The nail of flesh against the heart. A God of shape, transparency, and surface. Horrified by the bloodstream, and frightened by its throbbing, they sought the tranquility of agates and the shadowless nudity of the jellyfish.

When I entered the cathedral, they were singing the lamentation of six thousand virgins, which sounded and resounded under the three arches, full of tackle, waves and ropes, like three battles of Lepanto. The eye of the Saint gazed out of the tray with the cold sadness of an animal having just suffered the mortal knife thrust.

Space and Distance. Vertical and horizontal. Relation between you and me. Eyes of Santa Lucía! The veins in the soles of her feet slept outstretched in their rosy beds, soothed and illuminated from above by two little stars. We leave our eyes on the surface, like aquatic flowers, and hide, crouched up behind them, while our palpitating physiology floats through a dark world.

I went down kneeling.

The precentors were firing shots from the choir.

Meanwhile, night had arrived. Night, sealed in and brutal, like the head of a mule with leather blinkers.

In one of the exits hung the skeleton of an ancient fish; in the other, the skeleton of a seraph softly swayed by the ovalized air from the optical signs, smelling freshly of apples and the sea shore.

I was getting hungry and asked for my rooming house.

"You're now quite a distance from it. Don't forget that the cathedral is near the railway station and your house is toward the South, farther down the river."

"I have time to spare."

The railway station was nearby.

A wide square, symbolizing frustrated emotion lugged by the waning moon, opened in the background, tight as three o'clock in the morning.

Gradually, the eyeglasses were hidden in their small coffins of leather and nickel in the silence which reveals the subtle relation between fish, star and spectacles.

He who has seen his pince-nez isolated under the moonlight or who has abandoned his lorgnettes on the beach has understood, as I, that delicate harmony (fish, star and spectacles) which collides on a huge white tablecloth just moistened with champagne.

I could compose perfectly as many as eight still-lifes with the eyes of Santa Lucía.

The eyes of Santa Lucía, on the clouds, in the foreground, in an atmosphere from which birds have just flown.

The eyes of Santa Lucía, on the sea, on the face of a clock, on the sides of an anvil, on the large trunk recently cut off.

They can be compared with the desert, with large untouched surfaces, a foot of marble, a thermometer, an ox.

You cannot compare them with a mountain, a distaff, a toad, or with cotton goods. The eyes of Santa Lucía.

Removed from all throbbing and all affliction. Permanent. Immobile. Without the least flutter. Seeing how all surrounding things escape in their own difficult, eternal temperature. Worthy of the tray which gives them reality, and uplifted like the breasts of Venus confronting the monocle full of irony which the evil enemy employs.

I set out again, impelled by my gum-soled shoes.

Encircled by grand pianos, I was topped by a magnificent silence.

In the dark, etched out by electric bulbs, one could read without any effort at all: *San Lázaro's Station.*

San Lázaro was born extremely pale. He gave off the odor of a wet sheep. When they whipped him, he released little lumps of sugar from the mouth. He was sensitive to the least sound. Once he confessed to his mother that he could count in the morning, by their throbs, every heart in the village.

He had a predilection for the silence of another world which attracts fish; and always, passing through an arch, he bent his head low, terrified. After his resurrection, he invented the coffin, the wax taper, magnesium lights and railway stations. When he died, he was as hard and laminated as a silver loaf of bread. His soul limped behind, long since deflowered by that other world, and full of boredom, a narcissus in the hand.

The mail train had departed at midnight.

I had to leave on the express at two in the morning.

Entrances to cemeteries and platforms.

The same atmosphere, the same emptiness, the same broken glasses.

The rails receded, beating in their perspective of theorems, dead and outstretched like the arms of Christ on the Cross.

From the shadowy roofs fell stiff apples of fear.

In a neighboring tailor shop scissors were incessantly cutting pieces of white thread.

Cloth to cover everything from the shriveled bosom of the old woman to the cradle of the new-born child.

From behind, another traveler arrived. A single traveler.

He wore a white summer suit with pearl buttons and a duster of the same color. Under his newly cleaned panama shone his large death-subdued eyes, and between, his chiseled nose.

His right hand was made of hard plaster and he held, suspended from his arm, a basket of willows and chicken eggs.

I had no desire to speak with him.

He seemed preoccupied and as though expecting someone to call him. He was protected from his sharp pallor by a long beard, a beard which was the mourning for his own passing.

An extremely real and mortal symbol drew its initials in nickel on my tie.

That night was the very holiday eve in which all Spain crowded the railings to see a black bull look melancholic at the sky and roar every four minutes.

The traveler was in a country which suited him and in a night favoring his desire for perspectives, awaiting only the crack of dawn to fly in pursuit of those voices which must necessarily call out.

The Spanish night, night of drawn blood and iron nails, barbaric night, with breasts flung out to the air, surprised by a single telescope, pleased the frozen traveler. He liked its incredible depth where the plummet breaks and he took pleasure in immersing his feet in the bed of ashes and burning sand on which he rested.

The traveler strolled down the platform with the logic of a fish in the water or a fly in the air; he went back and forth without noticing the long sad parallels of those who wait for trains.

I pitied him greatly because I knew that he was hanging on a voice, and to hang on a voice is like being seated on the guillotine of the French Revolution.

A stab in my shoulder, an unexpected telegram, surprise. Until the wolf falls through the trap, he is unafraid. He enjoys the silence and likes the beating of the veins. But to expect surprise is to convert an always fleeting moment into a large purple glove that endures and fills the whole night.

The sound of the train came in confused as a whiplashing.

I grabbed my trunk while the man in the white suit looked in all directions.

Finally, from the neck of an authoritative loud-speaker, a clear voice rang out in back of the station. "Lázaro! Lázaro! Lázaro!" And the traveler began to trot, docile, full of unction, until he was lost among the last station lights. The moment I heard the voice crying "Lázaro! Lázaro! Lázaro!" my mouth was filled with fig marmalade.

I have been home only a few minutes.

Not in the least surprised, I have discovered my valise empty. Only a pair of goggles and a very white duster—two themes of a journey. Pure and isolated. The goggles on the table, raised to a maximum their concrete construction and superior reality. The duster, fainted in the chair in its perpetual last attitude, with a distance still somewhat human, a below-zero distance of the drowned fish. The goggles, inclined to a geometric theorem of exact demonstration, and the duster, thrown into a sea full of shipwrecks and sudden green splendors. Goggles and duster. On the table and across the chair. Santa Lucía and San Lázaro.

Chimera

CAST

Enrique   Old Man
Woman   Girl

Voices

(A door)

ENRIQUE: Good bye.

SIX VOICES *(inside):* Good bye.

ENRIQUE: I'll be away in the hills a long time.

VOICE: A squirrel.

ENRIQUE: Yes, a squirrel for you and also five birds which no child has ever had before.

VOICE: No, I want a lizard.

VOICE: And I want a mole.

ENRIQUE: Children, that's very discriminating of you. I'll bring everything you ask for.

OLD MAN: Very discriminating.

ENRIQUE: What's that?

OLD MAN: Shall I carry your bags?

ENRIQUE: No.

(The children's laughter is heard.)

OLD MAN: They're your children?

ENRIQUE: Six of them.

OLD MAN: I've known their mother, your wife, a long time. I was coachman in her father's house, but to tell the truth, now I'm little more than a beggar. The horses—ha! ha! Nobody knows how much horses scare me. May lightning strike their eyes! It's very hard to drive a coach. Awfully hard! If you're not afraid, don't touch it, but if you do, don't be afraid. Damn those horses!

ENRIQUE *(picking up his bags):* Leave me alone.

OLD MAN: No, no. For a little change, whatever you can spare, I'll carry them for you. It'll please your wife. She wasn't afraid of horses. She's happy.

ENRIQUE: Let's go, then. I must make the six o'clock train.

OLD MAN: Oh, the train! That's another story. Trains are nothing at all. If I lived a hundred years I wouldn't be scared of them. There's no life to them. They come and go. . . . But horses, now. . . . Look.

WIFE *(from the window):* Enrique darling, Enrique. Keep writing me. Don't forget me.

OLD MAN: Oh, that girl! *(laughing)* Remember how he used to scale the walls and climb those trees just to see you?

WIFE: I'll remember it till I die.

ENRIQUE: So will I.

WIFE: I'll be waiting for you. Good bye.

ENRIQUE: Good bye.

OLD MAN: Have no fear. She's your wife and she loves you. And you love her. Have no fear.

ENRIQUE: Yes, but this being apart worries me.

OLD MAN: There are worse things. What's worse is that things go right on and rivers keep running. What's worse is, maybe there'll be a cyclone.

ENRIQUE: I don't like your jokes. You're always at it.

OLD MAN: Ha-ha-ha! Everyone, and you especially, believes the big thing about a cyclone is the destruction it leaves. But for me, just the opposite. The big thing about a cyclone is. . .

ENRIQUE *(annoyed):* Let's go. It'll be six o'clock any minute.

OLD MAN: And then there's the ocean. . . . In the ocean. . .

ENRIQUE *(angry):* Let's go, I said!

OLD MAN: You haven't forgotten anything, have you?

ENRIQUE: I've left everything in perfect shape. Besides, what business is it of yours? The worst thing in the world is an old servant, a beggar.

VOICE 1: Papa.

VOICE 2: Papa.

VOICE 3: Papa.

VOICE 4: Papa.

VOICE 5: Papa.

VOICE 6: Papa.

OLD MAN: Your children.

ENRIQUE: My children.

GIRL *(in the doorway):* I don't want the squirrel. If you bring me a squirrel, I won't love you. Don't bring me a squirrel. I don't want it.

VOICE: And I don't want the lizard.

VOICE: And I don't want the mole.

GIRL: We want you to bring us a collection of minerals.

VOICE: No, no. I want my mole.

VOICE: No, the mole is mine...

(They quarrel.)

GIRL *(entering):* Well, now the mole belongs to me!

ENRIQUE: Enough! Be satisfied!

OLD MAN: You said they're very discriminating.

ENRIQUE: Yes. Very discriminating. Fortunately.

OLD MAN: How's that?

ENRIQUE *(loudly):* Fortunately.

OLD MAN *(sadly):* Fortunately.

(They leave.)

WIFE *(in the window):* Good bye.

VOICE: Good bye.

WIFE: Come back soon.

VOICE *(far away):* Soon.

WIFE: He'll cover himself well at night. He has taken four blankets. But I'll be alone in bed. I'll be cold. His eyes are wonderful, but I really love his strength.

(She undresses.)

My shoulder is a little sore. Oh, if he'd only hate me! I'd like him to hate me...but he loves me. I want to run away and have him catch me. I want him to burn me...burn me. *(aloud):* Good bye. Good bye...Enrique, Enrique...I love you. I see you growing small. You're jumping over the rocks. So small. Now I could swallow you like a button. I could swallow you, Enrique...

GIRL: Mama.

WIFE: Don't go out. A cold wind has come up. I said no!

(She comes out.)

(Light vanishes from the stage.)

GIRL *(speaking quickly):* Papaaa! Papaaa! Bring me a squirrel. I don't want the minerals. Minerals will break my fingernails. Papaaa!

BOY *(in the doorway):* He...doesn't...hear...you! He...doesn't...hear...you! He...doesn't...hear...you!

GIRL: Papa, I want the squirrel!

(breaking into tears)

Oh, God! I want the squirrel!

Dialogue of Amargo

CAST

Young Man 1   Amargo

Young Man 2   A Voice

Rider

(In the Countryside)

A VOICE: Amargo.
       The rosebays of my patio.
       Heart of bitter almond.
       Amargo.

(Three YOUNG MEN *in wide-brimmed hats enter.)*

YOUNG MAN 1: We're going to be late getting there.

YOUNG MAN 2: Night has overtaken us.

YOUNG MAN 1: What about him?

YOUNG MAN 2: He's lagging behind.

YOUNG MAN 1 *(loudly):* Amargo!

AMARGO *(far off):* I'm coming.

YOUNG MAN 2 *(yelling):* Amargo!!

AMARGO *(calmly):* Coming!

      (pause)

YOUNG MAN 1: What wonderful olive orchards!

YOUNG MAN 2: Yes.

      (long silence)

YOUNG MAN 1: I don't like walking about at night.

YOUNG MAN 2: Me either.

YOUNG MAN 1: Night was made for sleeping.

YOUNG MAN 2: True enough.

      (Frogs and crickets comprise the bower of the Andalusian summer. AMARGO *is walking, hands on hips.)*

AMARGO: Ay yayaya.
    Of Death I asked a question.
    Ay yayaya.

(The cry in his song has put a circumflex accent on the heart of those who've heard him.)

YOUNG MAN 1 *(from very far away):* Amargo!

YOUNG MAN 2 *(almost vanished):* Amargooo!

(AMARGO is alone in the middle of the road. He half-closes his big green eyes and wraps his corduroy jacket around him. High mountains surround him. His big silver watch ticks obscurely in his pocket at every step. A RIDER comes galloping down the road.)

RIDER *(stopping his horse):* Good evening!

AMARGO: Go with God.

RIDER: You going to Granada?

AMARGO: I go to Granada.

RIDER: So. We'll go together.

AMARGO: Seems so.

RIDER: Why not mount behind me?

AMARGO: Because my feet are not sore.

RIDER: I come from Malaga.

AMARGO: Good.

RIDER: That's where my brothers are.

AMARGO *(peevishly):* How many?

RIDER: Three of them. They sell knives. It's their business.

AMARGO: Hope it does them some good.

RIDER: Silver and gold.

AMARGO: A knife shouldn't be any more than a knife.

RIDER: You're wrong.

AMARGO: Thanks.

RIDER: Gold knives are meant just for the heart. Silver knives cut the throat like a blade of grass.

AMARGO: Aren't they used to cut bread?

RIDER: Men break bread with their hands.

146

AMARGO: True enough!

(*The horse shies.*)

RIDER: Horse!

AMARGO: It's the night.

(*The undulating road cavorts with the animal's shadow.*)

RIDER: You want a knife?

AMARGO: No.

RIDER: Look, a gift from me.

AMARGO: But I'm not taking it.

RIDER: You won't get another chance.

AMARGO: Who knows?

RIDER: Other knives are no good. Others are soft and afraid of blood. Those we sell are cold. Understand? They feel their way to the hottest spot, and stop right there.

(AMARGO *says nothing. His right hand grows cold as ice as if he'd grabbed a piece of gold.*)

RIDER: Such a beautiful knife!

AMARGO: Worth a lot?

RIDER: So wouldn't you like this one?

(*He pulls out a gold one. Its tip glistens like an open oil lamp.*)

AMARGO: I said no.

RIDER: Come, boy, get up here behind me!

AMARGO: I'm still not tired!

(*The horse shies again.*)

RIDER (*pulling the reins*): Well, what a horse!

AMARGO: It's the dark.

(*pause*)

RIDER: As I was telling you, my three brothers in Malaga have a real knack for selling knives! In the cathedral two thousand knives were bought to adorn all the altars and crown the tower. Crews on lots of ships engrave their names on the knives. The humblest fishermen on the seacoast find their way at night by the light their sharpened blades throw off.

AMARGO: It's a real beauty!

RIDER: Who would deny it?

> (*The night thickens like a century-old wine. The fat serpent of the South opens its eyes in early dawn and sleepers are full of an infinite yearning to throw themselves off the balcony into the perverse magic of perfume and the far-away.*)

AMARGO: I think we've lost our way.

RIDER (*stopping his horse*): Yes?

AMARGO: Because we were talking.

RIDER: Aren't those the lights of Granada?

AMARGO: I don't know. The world is very large.

RIDER: And very lonely.

AMARGO: As it is deserted.

RIDER: You said it.

AMARGO: It just fills me with despair. Ay yayaya!

RIDER: Because once you get there, what will you do?

AMARGO: What will I do?

RIDER: And if you were to be where you belong, why would you want to be there?

AMARGO: Why?

RIDER: I ride this horse and sell knives, but if I didn't, what would happen?

AMARGO: What would happen?

> (*pause*)

RIDER: We're coming into Granada.

AMARGO: Is it possible?

RIDER: See how the belvederes glisten!

AMARGO: Yes, they certainly do.

RIDER: Now you won't refuse to get up behind me.

AMARGO: Wait a moment.

RIDER: Come on, jump on. Climb up fast. We've got to get there before day breaks. And take this knife. A gift from me!

AMARGO: Ay yayaya!

(The RIDER *helps* AMARGO *up. They follow the road to Granada together. In the background the hills are covered with cactus and nettles.)*

Song of Amargo's Mother

They carry him wrapped in my sheet,
my rosebays and palm leaves.

On August twenty-sixth,
with a little gold knife.

The cross. And now it's done.
He was swarthy, and a bitter one.

Pass the lemonade, neighbor,
Out of your brass jar.

The cross. Don't weep, anyone.
Amargo is in the moon.

Episode of the Lieutenant Colonel
of the Civil Guard

CAST

Lieutenant Colonel   Voice
Sergeant   Gypsy
        Civil Guards

(Headquarters with flags)

LT. COL.: I am the Lieutenant Colonel of the Civil Guard.

SERGEANT: Yes.

LT. COL.: Which nobody can deny.

SERGEANT: No.

LT. COL.: I wear three stars and twenty crosses.

SERGEANT: Yes.

LT. COL.: The archbishop greets me with his twenty-four purple tassels.

SERGEANT: Yes.

LT. COL.: I am the Lieutenant. I am the Lieutenant. I am the Lieutenant Colonel of the Civil Guard.

(Romeo and Juliet, in sky-blue, white, and gold, embrace in the tobacco garden of the cigar box. The soldier caresses the long end of his gun which is full of submarine shadows. A voice is heard outside.)

VOICE: Moon, moon, moon, moon
    of olive time.
    Cazórla shows her tower
    and Benamejí hides it.

    Moon, moon, moon, moon.
    A cock crows in the moon.
    O, mayor, sir, your daughters
    are looking at the moon.

LT. COL.: Who goes there?

SERGEANT: A gypsy!

(The little GYPSY's young-mule's glance darkens and pops the beady eyes of the LIEUTENANT COLONEL of the Civil Guard.)

LT. COL.: I am the Lieutenant Colonel of the Civil Guard.

SERGEANT: Yes.

LT. COL.: And who are you?

GYPSY: A gypsy.

LT. COL.: And what is a gypsy?

GYPSY: Anything at all.

LT. COL.: What's your name?

GYPSY: Just that.

LT. COL.: What?

GYPSY: Gypsy.

SERGEANT: I ran into him and brought him along.

LT. COL.: Where were you?

GYPSY: On the bridge over the rivers.

LT. COL.: What rivers?

GYPSY: All rivers.

LT. COL.: And what were you doing there?

GYPSY: Building a tower of cinnamon.

LT. COL.: Sergeant!

SERGEANT: At your command, my Lieutenant Colonel of the Civil Guard.

GYPSY: I have invented wings to fly, so I fly. Sulphur and rose on my lips.

LT. COL.: Ay!

GYPSY: Though I don't need wings, because I fly without them. Clouds and rings in my blood.

LT. COL.: Ayy!

GYPSY: In January, I have orange blossoms.

LT. COL. (squirming): Ayyyy!

GYPSY: And oranges in the snow.

LT. COL.: Ayyyyyy! Bing, bang, boom.

(Falls dead.)

(The tobacco-and-coffee-and-cream soul of the LIEUTENANT COLONEL *of the Civil Guard departs through the window.)*

SERGEANT: Help!

(In the patio of headquarters, four Civil Guards are whipping the GYPSY.*)*

Song of the Whipped Gypsy

Twenty-four blows on the face
twenty-four blows on the face;
later, at night, my mother
will wrap me in silver paper.

You, Civil Guard passing there,
give me a few drops of water.
Water with boats and fishes,
water, water, water, water.

O, you Civil Guard boss,
you up there in your room—
there won't be enough silk kerchiefs
to wipe the blood off my face.

SOURCES AND NOTES

These translations derive from early versions I attempted: first as "Some Little Known Writings of Federico García Lorca," in *New Directions 1944, Number Eight*, 359–407, 1944, and *García Lorca*, 1944, both books by New Directions, Norfolk and New York; and again in *Divan and Other Writings*, Copper Beech Press, Providence, 1977. For the present book, I have revised all of my earlier translations, and also added the following new material: *The Billy-Club Puppets: Tragicomedy of Don Cristóbal and Mistress Rosita (Los títires de Cachiporra: Tragicomedia de don Cristóbal y seña Rosita); Cristobical (Cristobical);* and *The Girl Who Waters the Basil and the Inquisitive Prince (La niña que riega la albahaca y el príncipe preguntón).*

The Spanish texts from which the translations were made include *Obras completas*, edited by Guillermo de Torre, Losada, Buenos Aires, Vol. I, 1938, and Vol. VI, 1938; *Obras completas*, edited by Arturo del Hoyo, Aquilar, Madrid, Vol. II, 1986, and Vol. I, 1974; "Cristobical," edited by Piero Menarini, *Anales de Literatura Española Contemporánea*, 21–37, Boulder, Colorado, 1986; *Federico García Lorca (1898–1936)*, edited by Ángel del Rio, Hispanic Institute, New York, 1941; *El público y Comedia sin título*, edited by R. Martínez Nadal and M. Laffranque, Editorial Seix Barral, Barcelona, 1978.

Christopher Maurer, the "perfect-pitch" *lorquista*, made it possible for me to reimagine García Lorca's work in the 1990s and to fall in love again with the poet I had "discovered" and written about fifty years earlier. He has spurred the new effort made here to bring together in one place Lorca's four puppet plays. Professor Maurer also kept me from newly committing or repeating atrocious errors, frequent among "committed" translators, and to encourage my making leaps where necessary, and which I now trust never to regret.

John Emigh, theatre man and valued colleague, favored me with insights into the text of the *Billy-Club Puppets,* which he had been delving into in Madrid as early as 1961.

Old debts of gratitude are here recalled for the luminous counsel and spirit of the late Professors Ángel del Rio and Francisco García Lorca, and for the support and friendly enterprise of James Laughlin, who in 1943 agreed to publish my early translations as well as my book, *García Lorca.*

E.H.